Grandad's Old Clock

Poems & Memories

SECOND EDITION

Michael Breuleux

Copyright © 2025 Michael Breuleux

All rights reserved. No part of this publication in print or in electronic format may be reproduced, stored in a retrieval system, or transmitted in any form or by any means, electronic, mechanical, photocopying, recording, or otherwise without the prior written permission of the publisher.

The scanning, uploading, and distribution of this book without permission is a theft of the author's intellectual property. Thank you for your support of the author's rights.

Design and distribution by Bublish, Inc.

SECOND EDITION

ISBN: 978-1-647048-20-4 (hardcover)
ISBN: 978-1-647048-19-8 (eBook)

for

Mary Elizabeth Breuleux

1945–2016

the girl with the "pioneer spirit"

"How do I love thee? Let me count the ways.
I love thee to the depth and breadth and height
My soul can reach, when feeling out of sight
For the ends of being and ideal grace. . . ."

Sonnets from the Portuguese, No. 43
Elizabeth Barrett Browning
(1806–1861)

Table of Contents

Preface and Acknowledgments (2nd edition) xiii
Preface and Acknowledgments (1st edition) xv

Grandad's Old Clock

Grandad's Old Clock 3
Flight 93 (the 40) 12
A Chance Encounter 18
Blossomed Trees 20
Emma Rae 21
Cat Paws 22
Poetry & Mary Oliver 23
haiku 24
Fate of the Bonney Dourne 27
the Path 30
The Writer 32
Stephen Hawking tries to put God in a box 34
Words Spoken and Unspoken 35
of Wisdom 36
Ukraine's Children 38
Heather Henry's House 40

Poems by Friends

Smith Mountain Lake (Ken Henry) 43
Sonnet, to an Ancient Oak (Jess Roberts) 45
Ashes on the Ground (Ruth Wheaton) 46
Redemption (Claudia Hamm) 48
Radiance (Elizabeth Aires) 50
Mer-man (Joanne Wilson) 52
Mendocino (Joanne Wilson) 53
Marriage (Hi-Dong Chai) 54
Fifty Years (Kathy Cusick) 55
She Smiled (Roberta Bondelie) 56

Poems for Guys

Cigars & Beer 58
Limericks 60
'9ers and Bucs 62
Honey Badger 64
Capt'n Morgan & Wailer (Morgan's Oath) 66

Silly Stuff

Froggie, Froggie 70
Cookie, Cookie 71
Rub-a-dub-dub 72
95032 73
23059 73
Tink and Hook 74
Duck vs. Tree 76

Nosey Mouse

Fun Fair for the Forest Friends (Mayme "Mimi" Frommeyer)............78
The Adventures of Ginger & Candy (Mayme "Mimi" Frommeyer)....81

Holidays

No Santa Claus!...86
No Santa Claus?..87
Snow Bound (a Christmas Holiday)...89
Christmastide Angel...92
Christmas Peace..94
Looking at a Ringed Moon on New Year's Eve...............................96

for Mary

I Understood...100
Everything..101
The Rose..102
I Wondered as I Wandered..103
Mary's Song...105
Reflections on a Himalayan Urn...109
Beloved..111
Parsley, Sage, Rosemary & Thyme..112
Living Water..114
Living Water (a sonnet)...115
I AM 116
Father, we thank You . . . (Rebecca J. Weston, 1885)..................119
O Love!..121
The Shepherd's Prayer...122
You Restore My Soul..125

The Vineyard

Springtime Vineyard 130
Summertime's Vineyard 131
Claire's Field in Autumn 132
Winter Vineyard 133

On Sea Ranch (Lawrence Halprin, 1964) 135
I don't hike the trail until I'm invited. 136
On the Kingdom of God, an Open Bible and My Dad 137
I had a dream 140
Godspeed 142

Endnotes 145
Photo Credits and Notes 159

Preface and Acknowledgments
(Second edition)

The second edition of *Grandad's Old Clock* introduces some new poems. A new chapter, "Holidays," is included; a second children's story written by my grandmother, Mimi, lengthens the chapter dedicated to her; and Endnote 4b has been rewritten.

I thank the following for their editorial help and opinions as well as their comments that improved some of these poems: Rex Allen, Alice Bailey, Susan Black Sweeting, Betty Blote, Pete Breuleux, Darla Ferreira, Kim Ferreira, Claudia Hamm, Ken Henry, John Lococo, Sandi Lococo, Jack Longley, Cindy McCalmont, Pat Mulcaire, Fred Oliver, Lizanne Oliver, Les Pederson, Jeanette Rapp, Joanne Wilson.

Thanks Bet and Pete for your help with Mimi's stories. Thank you again Shilah of Bublish, Inc. for your professional help with the second edition of *Grandad's Old Clock*.

Michael Breuleux
Los Gatos, California, 2024

Preface and Acknowledgments
(First edition)

This book is not so much a book of poems as it is a short *memoir* that sketches in part my memories and life with Mary, my wife—the girl I married fifty years ago. Thank you, Shirley Sturdivant, a good friend, for giving me Don Blanding's book *Joy Is an Inside Job*.[1] Blanding used his poems and short essays and art to tell his late-in-life story of how he found peace and joy. I've used the format of Blanding's book as a guide. Most of my book includes poems I have written, but the reader will also find some short prose as well as photographs that friends and I have taken. I hope the content of my book reflects the deep feeling and love I have for Mary.

Perhaps readers will find a poem they like. If they do, that would be nice; but if no poem is found, that's okay too. Poetry is an individual "thing," and different people prefer different forms of verse. A good friend once aptly remarked, "Poetry is the *jazz* of writing;"[2] and it comes to us in many different forms. Some forms follow strict "rules," while other forms do not—from the old Shakespearian sonnet of precisely 140 syllables set in fourteen lines of rhymed iambic pentameter to the modern reverso poem. I tend to write "old school," and many of my poems rhyme. Much "modern poetry," written in free verse, does not rhyme (and we can thank Walt Whitman for that). I've tried to write some modern poetry too. Hopefully, I've achieved a small degree of success.

Some of these poems reflect the spiritual sense I have about God. This sense has been influenced in no small part by the gifted ministers who spiritually guided Mary and me. We were privileged over the years to have known ministers who possessed both the gift of pastoral care and the skill of preaching. As such, I thank the following pastors and preachers of Stone Church of Willow Glen: Rev. Dr. Bob Bowles, Rev. Dr. Art Mills, Rev. Rebecca Kuiken, Rev. Dr. Ken Henry, Rev. Irene Pak Lee, and Rev. Jim Bender.

More recently for me, I thank the following pastors and preachers of the Presbyterian Church of Los Gatos: Rev. Dr. David Watermulder, Rev. Erica Rader, and Rev. Jack Longley. Thank you Chaplain Chris Belluomini, former chaplain of The Terraces of Los Gatos, for your pastoral care and support.

I thank the members of The Book Club for the support and love they gave Mary and for the example they set by the love and support they gave each other. Their example, whether they know it or not, influenced my perception of *agape* love and is reflected in some of these poems. Mary's friends and The Book Club were very important to Mary. So I thank, Lizanne Oliver, Sandi Lococo, Jenefer Curtis, and Alice Bailey. A photograph of The Book Club can be found on page 104.

My thanks to Lynden Keith Johnson, artist and good friend, for painting the acrylic, *Stengel Beach at Sea Ranch, California's Mendocino Coast*. A copy of the painting can be found on page 107. Sea Ranch was a very special place for Mary and me and it remains so for me.[3]

Thank you Jeanette Rapp, Renaissance woman and good friend, for your friendship, calligraphy, graphic art, and your very helpful editorial insights. Thank you so much Claudia Hamm for your poetry, for your friendship, and for the support and love you gave Mary.

My sincere thanks to Melody Casagranda, Mary's twin sister; Sue Perez, Mary's youngest sister; and Darla and Kim Ferreira, Mary's and my nieces, for your editorial opinions and help.

A special thank-you to Betty Blote, my sister, and Betty Sosaya, Bet's friend and next-door neighbor, for their editorial opinions and poetry. Thank you, Bet, for your help with Mimi's story. My thanks to Pete Breuleux, my brother, and Pat Blote, my brother-in-law for their editorial help and opinions.

Thank you to my good friend Ed Shaw for the motivation and encouragement you gave me to complete this book. I always looked forward to our morning coffees and conversation, and I miss them. You made my life richer.

I would be remiss if I did not acknowledge and thank my friends and fellow poets who allowed me to publish their poems. Their names and poems can be found in the chapter entitled "Poems by Friends."

Thank you Kathy Meis, Founder and CEO of Bublish, Inc., Mount Pleasant, South Carolina and the Bublish team for bringing my book to life. Thank you Shilah for your professionalism, creativity and for your patience.

Much prayer preceded and followed this short book. Admittedly though, I tend to procrastinate—a characteristic that caused at times some friction between Mary and me. So I can well put off today what I can do tomorrow. Unfortunately, tomorrow never comes. So I thank Jesus the Christ for pushing me along the path to complete this book. Without His help, my book never would have been written.

M.B.
Los Gatos, California, 2022

Grandad's Old Clock

Michael Breuleux

Grandad's Old Clock[4]

Grandad's Old Clock—you've bless'd our home,
As Time traveled your lyric chime;
Fam'ly graced by your deep *shalom*—
As through the years you've marked the time.

Gift to Dad on his engagement—
Married to Mom with deepen'd love,
Shar'd together with endearment;
Family's bond of care and love.

For Grandad gifted unto Dad
Grandad's Old Clock for fam'ly dear,
Legacy to daughter and lad—
Faithful stewards through day and year.

How rich the sound of *Grandad's Clock*,
How golden is your ticking sound,
Poetic is your chime unlocked
To all who listen well—unbound.

Crafted of oak—solid and brown,
And burnished brass you do display,
Finished wood to a rich nut-brown,
A face of brass—white tile inlaid.

Fair maid and Cupid hidden well
Behind the swinging pendulum;
But will the hidden arrow's spell
Make near her lover's kiss as won?

Good maid, why dost hold Cupid's bow
And disregard a plaintive plea?
Your answer, to protect your beau,
Or perchance keep what you've agreed?

The *Old Clock's* brass pendulum swings
To the rhythms of Silent Time,
On its face, cherubs play and sing
Alluring songs of riddled rhyme.

What pipes—what lyre—do cherubs play—
Haunting melodies to a muse?
As journeyed through a forest way,
Astride a noble beast bemused.

What story does your turret hold?
Of anointed lad perhaps—through,
An age of war and troop so bold—
Mythic history to review?

Wisdom surveys atop your crown
GOD's Creation that stirs below,
Creative vastness all but found,
In Wisdom's Force that She would know.

What tales, what stories—grand and small
You, *Old Clock*, could recite to us—
To those who listen to your call,
What you could tell—for tell you must!

Charm'd are we by this noble clock,
But are we chain'd by Time so bound?
For Time, O Time, do you but mock,
Prisoned we to your silent sound?

Silent Time how should you be known?
A gift as gold and frankincense;
Or wasted space that we but moan;
Or vile idol that dulls our sense?

Do you, Time, have but a brief history,
Your ancient wave found in a cosmic string—
Brief—gone—to evaporate—
And then no more?

Or are you eternal and have no beginning and no end,
Where you begin and end as one—
Bound together—to be—
And we but a circular illusion?

Time the beginning,
Time the end,
Time the infinite,
Time the infinitesimal.

Mortal then spoke,
"Time . . .
Bound in the Unified Complete Theory of Everything;[4a]
Once found, we will then know *What* the Universe is;
Then we will answer the question *Why* it is that we and the Universe exist;
We then . . .
TRIUMPHANT!
For this will be the ultimate triumph of human reason—
For then we will know the mind of God!"

GOD then spoke from beyond the depths of Time,
"Mortal . . .
Who has known the mind of GOD?
Who has directed the Spirit of the LORD?
Who has counseled YHWH?
    I created the Cosmos—seen and not seen—
    Out of what did not exist—*creatio ex nihilo.*
Who has known what did not exist?
Who was there when I created Wisdom?
Who?" . . . asks the LORD,
"Surely you know, for you were born then,
And the number of your days is great!"

Eugene Albert "Grandad" Frommeyer
Betty Rae and Jean
(Grandad's granddaughters)
Cincinnati, Ohio
circa 1939

"I AM . . .

before Creation . . .

before the cosmic beginning . . .

before and beyond the depths of Time . . .

beyond the infinite . . .

beyond Eternity . . .

I AM the A and the Ω . . . the Unbound

for . . .

I AM."

"Mortal . . .

You see in a mirror dimly—you look but through a glass shadowed and blurred,

For the Universe seen and not seen is but an infinitesimal measure of My Creation.

Beyond this universal plain . . . behind this cosmic curtain

Lies a creative vastness . . . a Mystery . . .

> far too wonderful—
>
> far too magnificent—
>
> far too fearfully beautiful—
>
> far too grand . . .

For mortal perception.

It is a high and holly Mystery—

It is a Mystery to wonder and search out with an awed and humbled heart;[4b]

Yet it is a Mystery beyond mortal reason of the *What*."

"Mortal know . . .

One and One and One are ONE;

Wisdom's Force transcends mortal reason;

two are as one;

there is a time for all things and that which is,

already has been—that which is to be, already is—

and I seek out that which has gone by;

some things are uncertain for you; yet to GOD all things are certain;[4c]

I AM in the vastness of My Creation for it is I who binds It—and yet—

I AM fully in those who seek the perfect *shalom* of My Word;

if you search for Me, you will find Me—if you seek

Me with a humbled heart."

Grandad's Old Clock chuckles at will,
For who can put GOD in a box?
Mortal's words are but spoken nil,
Cannot the mind of GOD unlock.

"To love the LORD leads to the *Why*,
Heart and mind and will all given,
Soul and self to GOD lifted high,
Might of one's devotion driven."

"To know the *Why* one then must cede:
Love your neighbor as you yourself,
Bring love more, yet to those in need—
The Law's Commandments thus upheld."

Grandad's Old Clock keeps Silent Time
As the *Old Clock* messages well.
And the *Old Clock* rings loud its chime:
GOD's Creation cannot be quelled.

As the Pendulum of Time swings,
Waves of Time move through the ages;
And Times' rivers together sing
Of Creation new but aged.

Michael Breuleux

Flight 93[5]

(the 40)

I

Listen, my friends, to a story told,
Of heroes lost long ago—of everyday folk—O so bold;
Men and women like you and me,
Women and men and just plain folk—heroes all on Flight 93.
On 9/11, Two-thousand-one, a date which lives in infamy,
Our nation lost patriots brave, now heroes honored in history.

II

Forty Americans on a humdrum flight,
Newark to Frisco at the dawn's early light,
Mothers, mentors—fathers and friends,
Everyday folk of every stripe; people on whom we depend.
Todd Beamer was one of the 40 who died,
Seven comrades who stood by his side:
Welsh, Nacke, and Captain Dahl,
Glick, Bingham, Burnett, and Sandra Bradshaw.[5a]

III

The 40 boarded the flight with innocent thought,
For they knew not the evil the terrorists sought,

Four terrorists hijacked the plane midair,
Justice and Freedom they could not bear,
For Liberty's ring fell on deaf ear;
Four boiled with hatred and malice within,
And they sparked a war they would not win.

IV

On that murderous day in hell,
When aboard 93 the terrorists fell,
Four cowards to do Evil's work,
Of death and destruction—a scene berserk,
Innocents they had in mind,
To murder and maim in twisted time,
Cowards they were who cowered low,
'Neath a flame of courage on 93.

V

A call to arms the 40 heard,
A call they heard in a blaze of light,
And they steeled themselves for a mortal fight;
Beamer summoned the call by his fearless command:
"Are you guys ready? Okay, let's roll!"
Bingham echoed then a defiant shout:
"C'mon! Get 'em!! Get 'em!!!"—
A battle cry for all to hear;
Then roll they did, up the aisle they fought,
A heroic charge, striking mortal blows,
A defiant message to our terrorist foes.

VI

They charged the aisle, striking blow for blow,
A terrorist down and then brought low,
Hand to hand in the aisle they fought,
Strike on strike what chaos wrought!
Another down and the cockpit reached,
Blow for blow and the portal breached,
The final assault and victory!
Won by the heroes on 93.

VII

The airliner crashed that ominous day,
In the wooded hills near Shanksville, PA,
The Towers were hit and the Pentagon too,
Innocents murdered and friends we knew.
(Dark shadows of Pearl in '41,
And the heroes then who fought and won.)
Other murderous plans our foe devised,
The U.S. Capitol the terrorists prized,
But because of the courage on 93,
The courage of folk like you and me,
Our nation's Capital, our foe denied.

VIII

Forty heroes on a routine flight,
Their names now etched in history.
Husbands, wives, and everyday folk,
Rose up as one to battle the foe:
Beamer, Bingham, Burnett, and Dahl,

Nacke, Glick, Welsh, and Sandra Bradshaw;
Thirty-two others died aboard—heroes all on Flight 93.[5a]

IX

They struck the first blow at the terrorist foe in a global war declared,
When our souls were tried and our wills tested,
When our banner yet waved above rubble and smoke,
And heroes arose from everyday life,
When we stood together from prairie to sea,
When folks reached out to strangers as friends,
And together we stood—United as one!

X

In an earlier time and younger era,
When the fate of our nation hung in the balance and independence declared,
Patriots past of common folk rose up and kindled the flame:
Revere, Dawes, and Prescott[5]—their midnight rides revered,
Warned the folk of the countryside of the British march so near—
For on that eve—an echoed alarm—but not the alarm of fear.
Margaret Corbin—with shattered jaw and wounded breast,
Her canon thundered at the Hessian crest,
No braver patriot she, as our nation fought for Liberty.
And at the Old North Bridge stood farmers bold,
"And fired the shot heard 'round the world."
Thomas Paine wrote *The Crisis* and pled our Cause in *Common Sense*,
Those were the times that tried men's souls—for Freedom's Fight was intense.
Betsy Ross stitched—the Red and White and starry Blue,
The Stars and Stripes, forever held, high and true.

XI

So heed the lessons of history's past,
From deeds of valor done long ago,
By women and men like you and me,
By men and women like you and me,
Ordinary folk of every stripe,
But extraordinary heroes in everyday life,
Gave of themselves with nothing sought,
Heroes now in history's light.

XII

Never forget the heroes on 93!
When Beamer gave his fearless command,
A command of defiance and not of fear,
In the hallow'd tradition of Prescott, Dawes, and Revere;
Through all our history, dark storms have rolled,
But our people have met the challenge that tolled.
(Remember the heroes of '44—
Allies who fought on Normandy's shore?)

XIII

So now is the day to rise as one,
Now is the time to unite as before,
Now is the hour to obey the command:
"Are you guys ready? Okay, let's roll!"

Michael Breuleux
September 2016

A Chance Encounter[6]

Cold—
    as the fresh fallen snow.
        a High Sierra weekend,

Fast—
    as a carving ski.
        a change of scene,

High—
    as a snowy cornice.
        away from the madding crowd,

Cold and Swift—
    as an icy mountain waterfall.
        was all I hoped for;

Wild—
    as the gusty wind.
        and then I met her,

Warm—
>   as the afternoon sun.
>   >   a chance encounter,

Blue—
>   as the High Sierra sky.
>   >   on that ski trail,

White—
>   as a billowy cloud.
>   >   a look . . . a touch . . .

Clear—
>   as a chilly-cold mountain stream.
>   >   a moment . . .

Blue on Black—
>   as the stellar jay.
>   >   a spark!

Gray—
>   as the granite mountain.
>   >   and my life was changed,

Green—
>   as the Alpine fir.
>   >   never to be the same again.

Blossomed Trees

Among the blossomed trees we walked,
Little known the storm they'd bring,
Mantled high and covered low
With tufts of white . . . as white as snow,
For when the breeze would blow and sing,
A petal-blizzard stirred our walk.

O how we wished this jocund scene
Would remain throughout the year,
But alas, seasons come and seasons go,
And the tufts of white . . . as white as snow,
No more a blizzard to bring us cheer;
But come next spring, if we allow, again our blossomed-walk serene.

Emma Rae[7]

O sweet Emma Rae you came this day
    on a beautiful Sunday morn;
Happy are we as your star we see
    on the wonderful day you were born.

Know you are loved—by the LORD above—
    by your Mom and Dad and more;
We love you dear—GOD brought you here—
    and many counted the days afore.

The choices you make and the paths you take,
    let your guide be GOD's hallow'd hand,
Growing up you'll do and we'll see you through—
    your family and friends will stand.

Happy days will be and rainbows you'll see
    as you follow life's future paths;
You'll experience joys and days will poise
    the fun and adventure you'll have.

Strong you'll grow for this we know
    a woman of will and mind;
For the future will be who we will see
    a woman compassionate and kind.

In the adventure of life there will be strife,
    but Jesus will lead you through;
By His divine grace and His radiant face
    as He smiles and blesses you.

Michael Breuleux,
Emma's Uncle
August 2017

Cat Paws

The damp, drizzly fog creeps in
on silent cat paws.
She stops for a moment—
sits on gray haunches
and surveys the early morning Cove.
Satisfied—
all is well,
she moves inland to the Meadow beyond.

Stengel Beach Cove
Sea Ranch, Sonoma Coast
early morning, June 26, 2017

Poetry & Mary Oliver

I thought . . .
so this is how I should read poems,
not cover to cover,
but find ones that help me see a higher reality
—at least for the moment.
I read Mary Oliver,
for the first time,
the other day.
I like Mary Oliver.

She writes about her walks
—I guess around Provincetown—
about what she sees and what she hears,
and what she finds and what she feels.
I like Mary Oliver very much.

I'm told she takes a hand-sewn notebook with her
to write in,
(good advice for poets);
she forgot a pen one time
so she couldn't write,
so she hid wooden pencils in trees and bushes and such,
so that wouldn't happen again,
(good advice, again, I guess).
I like Mary Oliver.

Thank you Alice for this.

mola mola[8]

mola mola glides
ghost-like thru kelp'd green waters—
Monastery Beach

---

egret

egret—snow white, proud,
slow—foraging taro fields—
looks for little fish

monarch[8]

fair regal monarch,
black-orange wings touch the still air—
flower of the breeze

---

pelicans

brown pelicans—three,
formation—searching for fish,
skimming the Ocean

Fate of the Bonney Dourne

The clipper Bonney Dourne,
Had sailed the China Sea,
Now cargo laden for Frisco's port,
With a hardy crew of twenty-three.

From Boston Yard she sailed
South toward the Cape of Horn,
Little known to the proud ship's crew,
The fate of the Bonney Dourne.

South by south—then west by west—
She sailed Magellan Straits,
Into the Pacific's maw she ripped,
Toward Hell and Satan's Gates.

She rigged upon her masts,
Yards squared taut and true,
Rigging keen, ropes laid out,
And a rag of tops'l too.

With bow in spray and spumy foam,
'Neath the leaden sky,
The Bonney Dourne sliced the wave,
Oh how she could fly!

The crack of sail, the rage of sea,
Were heard all through the night;
Wild horses thundered by her side,
With nostrils flared red and white.

At eighty west and forty south,
As best as they could say,
A great wave crashed across her bow,
And cracked her mast away.

Wave on wave—sea on sea,
Came the mighty surge,
Gale winds stiffened, yardarms broke,
And mad black water could not be purged.

Swept to leeward, the boatswain's mate,
Lashed to a splintered rim,
Crashing water swept the deck,
And five lads followed him.

"Man the fores'ls—square the bracing!"
They heard the Captain shout;
The weighty waves roiled the deep,
And thrashed the Bonney Dourne about.

Lightening hissed the Southern Sky,
And lighted Satan's scene,
Seas boiled—waters raged—
In a cauldron of black and green.

At eighty west and forty south,
The Bonney Dourne went down,
All twenty-three, the proud ship too,
Heard no more a sound.

the Path

I'd climb every mountain for her,
Though the course be crooked and rough;
And if I knew the path to her heart,
I would surely take it.

I'd cross the sea for her,
Through rage of storm and gale,
To the ends of earth I'd follow,
Through desert and misty vale.

I'd walk the beach secluded,
And cross the river deep;
And if I knew the path to her heart,
I would surely take it.

I'll look for her 'mid the shadows
In the misty morning light—
I'll ponder and I'll think of her,
In the early morning light.

'Neath the honeysuckled arbor,
I'll wait for her and wonder—
Felt through my love and ardour
I'll wonder and I'll wait.

For her I'll hold a rose,
As I wait for morn's first light;
I'll give to her a rose,
'Mid the early morning's light.

At morning's dawn I'll see her,
The dawn that wakens her sleep,
Loving and thinking of her,
With the love my heart doth keep.

My heart doth surely tell
That I have loved her so;
And if I knew the path to her heart,
I would surely take it.

Once I truly asked,
"Do you really know? Do you know I care?"
She touched my cheek and gently smiled . . .
But silence was all she shared.

If I only knew,
If I knew she loved me;
If I knew the path to her heart,
I would surely take it.

The Writer

The old man sits with pen in hand,
Ink in well to fill the page,
An oil lamp burns the night away,
As shadows cast across the room.

In the old way, the old man writes,
For he feels the words belong to him;
As he crafts his work upon the page,
'Neath a crackling fire softly heard.

Outside, the chill of winter's night,
Snow on pane and glistening moon,
The old man turns and lends an ear,
To hear a snow owl's distant hoot.

A smile across his weathered face,
But back to work he must be,
With pen in hand and ink in well,
He begins to craft his story told.

Imagery, character and simple prose,
Make his writing come alive,
Reference to a shelved *Thesaurus*,
Yields the word to match his thought.

Carroll and Keats—Brontë and Byron,
Writers foremost of their craft,
A fleeting thought of their past,
Thoughts of them and their Guild.

Word by word his story builds,
Line by line his plot unfolds,
Simile, style and metaphor,
Make his prose come alive.

Characters reveal across the page:
The posh young maid with brunette hair,
Captures the heart of the pirate bold—
But will the reader believe this match?

Strunk & White by his side,
Reference to *The Elements of Style*,
"Get the little book!" his Prof. once said,
Oh, if were as easy as that!

Daylight comes—the lamp burns down,
The manuscript on wooden desk,
The old man frowns and turns a page,
Revision and edit on his mind.

Alas! . . . the writer's work is never done;
The writer's work is never done.

Stephen Hawking tries to put God in a box

Zech 8:6; Mk 10:27; Lk 1:37

Possible—
All things are
With God.
"You fool,"
Says Hawking,
"Impossible!"

~

"Impossible,"
Says Hawking.
You fool,
With God,
All things are
Possible!

Michael Breuleux

*(a "reverso poem"—
a poetry form invented by Marilyn Singer)*[9]

Whoever forgives seeks love.
Proverbs 17:9a

Words Spoken and Unspoken

A friend of hers angered her,
She turn'd her cheek and spoke to her,
She told her how it hurt within,
And forgave her friend for her sin,
Her anger left and dimmed within.

He was angered by a foe,
No word spoken—his hate did grow,
An angered rage filled his heart,
A hateful anger that would not part.

Jagged hate scream'd helter-skelter,
His angered heart beat skelter-helter,
Deceitful smiles did hide his rage,
No forgiveness to turn the page,
Nothing done to rid the rage.

One fateful night the two did chance,
Two lives set t'ward a struggled dance,
Angered hate remain'd unpurged,
Both heard that night a funeral dirge.

Michael Breuleux
Spring 2015

אני, חכמה, קיבלתי את שלום ה' המושלם

of Wisdom

1 Kings 3:3-14; Proverbs 8-9
The Wisdom of Solomon 6:12-22, 7:22-30; Sirach 1:1-10

I sing

I sing! O I sing to humanity,
    from the highest mountain top I sing,
        from the lowest ocean depth I sing.
            I sing for humanity to hear the *Song of Wisdom*.
            I sing for humanity to hear Her *Song*
        sung throughout Creation.
            O how I sing!

GOD's Creation

And GOD created Wisdom, the first of GOD's acts.
    And GOD spoke and it was done.
    And GOD saw that it was very good.

of Wisdom

The LORD created Me before the Beginning—
the first of the LORD's acts—
    Long before the Beginning was I brought forth.

    I was created before my four brothers. I am the first, yet I am the fifth. They are the architects, yet I am the reason. For it is I who counsels My brothers as the LORD guides Me.

I was beside the LORD and I was the LORD's delight. I received the perfect *Shalom of GOD* and it shone within me. I rejoiced in the work. I worked as a master artisan as I hewed the seven pillars and covered Creation like a mist.

O simple ones—O learned ones—O mighty ones—O humanity—
Listen to Me!

I speak of noble things; from my lips comes what is right, for my mouth speaks truth—

> From Me comes Justice and Equity and Dignity—strive for Me O humanity—strive for Me;
>
> I am the author of Beauty and Symmetry and Diophantine elegance—look for Me O humanity—look for Me in Creation;
>
> Faith and Compassion and Love emanate from Me; they are My beacons—be guided by Me O humanity—be guided by Me.

Wickedness and hate and lies are loathsome to Me; they disgust Me; and all who follow them follow Evil. Woe to those who follow these things.

I sing

I sing! O I sing to humanity,
   from the mountain tops I sing,
      from the ocean depths I sing.
         I sing for humanity to hear the *Song of Wisdom*.
         I sing for humanity to hear Her *Song*
         sung throughout Creation.
            O how I sing!

Ukraine's Children[10]

War rages across the Ukraine—
As Evil sweeps in from the East.
Little girls and boys . . . two, three and four
hold their mothers' hands and trudge westward
away from the thundering bombs,
the strike of missiles and the bomb-laden drones.
"Protected" by their teddy bears and *Raggedy Anns*
Children struggle to the West—and safety.
    Such is the madness of War.

Bombs thunder into Bakhmut
as waves of Wagner storm-troops ravage the city's streets.
A February snow falls and mixes with the mud and smoke and blood of War.
Missiles crater the once bustling city—as apocalypse nears.
A little girl looks into her grandfather's eyes and asks what is happening.
She too clutches her teddy bears for "protection"
as her life is shattered and her childhood stolen.
    Such is the horror of War.

From this madness—from this horror—we turn to You—
God of Peace.
Protect these children of the Ukraine from the bombs, the missiles—the bomb-laden drones;
Protect these children of the Ukraine from the Wagner storm-troops that ravage their city;
Have the children play under clear sky and white cloud as they did before and have the smoke and smolder of destruction be no more;
Have the children run in sunlight on mountain and meadow as they did before and have the bomb and bullet be no more.
God of Peace,
    we ask, protect these children.

This is all we ask, God of Peace—
    this is all we ask.

Michael Breuleux, 2023

Bakhmut, Ukraine
February 2023

Heather Henry's House

(an alliterative poem)

I was invited once . . .
To a house . . .
On Hester Street.
In fact, the house
On Hester Street,
Was Heather Henry's house.
A lovely, lively house it was,
That house on Hester Street—
With friends and folks in friendly conversation,
And trellised trees and flowered foliage
About the house.
A very pleasing, charming house it was,
Heather Henry's house on Hester Street.
And for a moment, I tarried some and mused the melodic melodies that
played from Heather Henry's music room—
A cozy, cool and comfy room
It was—
At the back of Heather Henry's house.
And I lingered a bit and said to myself,
"What a lively, lovely, house this is—
this house of Heather Henry's on Hester Street—
for I have a pleasing feeling here."

Poems by Friends

Smith Mountain Lake, Virginia
Photograph by Ken Henry, 2020

Smith Mountain Lake

I take my going slowly at Smith Mountain Lake.
A nearby squirrel cuts leaves for nesting material.
She repels downward, clinging to the vertical bark,
Carrying branches in her teeth and claws.
Half Dome is child's play for her.
No ropes, no harness, pure instinct.

A White Ash stands still, one leaf swinging like a pendulum.
I hear a splash; a warbler greets the grey morning sky;
The Red-Headed Woodpecker visits, briefly—
Rain is on the way.
Like me, it seems these woods are waiting for something:
A flash of lightning, a stiff wind, the inevitability of Fall.

My father is waiting, and we are waiting for him.
There must be moments like these for him:
Still moments, quiet moments,
Moments of the long ache,
The feeling that you're almost home.
An acorn hits the roof above my head,
Bringing me back to this life,
Reminding me to stay awake
To the impending seasons.

Ken Henry
Gearhart, Oregon

Sonnet, to an Ancient Oak

Great Mother Oak, how many centuries
have come and gone beneath your arching shade?
How many children splashed among your leaves,
how many mothers rested while they played?

Just so have I, soul-weary, settled down,
Your gnarled and knobbled trunk against my head,
The sunlight dappling through your twisting crown,
Your prickled leaves a disappointing bed,

And mused upon the multitudes you've blessed:
As landmark, shelter, guardian, or guide,
As fire or food, encouragement or rest,
As raptor's turret, rodent's home and hide.

And when you fall, by your decay you will,
even as shattered bones, keep blessing still.

Jess Roberts
Stone Church Women's Retreat–2019
St. Francis Retreat Center,
San Juan Bautista

Ashes on the Ground

The sun rose late in autumn skies.
As habit led, I pulled on shirt and boots
    and headed out the door.
Sweet and cool the morning air,
    and silent,
    save for calling quail
    and singing birds
    and rabbits on the run.
Urging me on, the trail led up
    across red rocks, through trees
    and cactus, bush and blooms.
The goal once more was *Sugar Loaf*,
    the mountain where I daily find a place
    of solitude and peace to start the day.
The distant view, familiar rocks on which I sit
    and ancient juniper awaited there.

But, Oh!, my eyes soon fell upon the ground,
    as there around the juniper were seen
Grey ashes in a circle spread,
And interspersed within, rose petals,
    red and dry, in tribute to a life.

A life!!—now only tiny bits of bone and flesh
    charred into dust.
What was this life? I know not age, or race
    or sex or creed.
Was this a mother, father, husband, wife,
    perhaps a child—but someone dear.
Someone who loved this mountain just like I.
But now the soul has flown to realms unknown.
And what remains are memories
    of words
    and deeds,
    and ashes on the ground.

Ruth Wheaton

Redemption

The path is long and far from smooth.

Along the way,

I stumble over *lust* and reveal *temperance*.

Farther along,
I trip over *gluttony* and reveal *generosity*.

Ahead,
I stub my toe on *greed* and reveal *benevolence*.

Soon,
I slip past *anger* and reveal *agreeability*.

Then,
I slide on the smoothness of *sloth* and reveal *vigor*.

Next,
I skid on *envy* and reveal *self-esteem*.

Finally,
I fall over *pride* and reveal *humility*.

At the path's end, it is revealed
that seven sins and their places,
have been redeemed by seven graces.

~ Claudia Hamm, 2015

Micah 6:8
He has told you, O mortal, what is good;
    and what does the Lord require of you
but to do justice, and to love kindness,
    and to walk humbly with your God?

Radiance

After days of silence, I gaze
into a pond—a reflection of rusts and golds—
and I remember a body I saw once
that became luminous before death.

I saw it—how the body gleamed,
smooth as burnished bark,
or polished stone tumbled by water,
sanded down and washed to shore.

She had known suffering, of course,
and it transformed her
from a child to a woman
and then it seemed into something more—

Before she took her last breath,
I witnessed the quietude
of letting go, of giving up
everything

until nothing was left, nothing
to cling to, only the heart
ajar, unbarred, wide
as the sky, and empty

as a moon's reflection
on the sea, a naked awareness
a kind of radiance, that shone
within her, a surfeit

of light, open as this pond
becomes full with color
and its deeper stones,
the surface rippling now

from a breeze that moves through
the tops of trees, then dies, the water
again a mirror of sky, liquid ambers,
the sheen of golden aspens,

the leaves that adhere and cling
to the delicate branches,
before the slow release—and then—
the letting go.

Elizabeth Aires

Under the sand,
    under the ocean
the mer-man sleeps.
He awakes at noon
and his curly-grey scales
and his sea-blue eyes
make love to the waves.

Joanne Wilson,
from "the Summer of Love"

Sheets of rain fell down,
mist swirled around the trees
   like angel hair;
occasionally a stark tree
intruded upon the grey.
Perched on a railing
a seagull looked to the wind
and dreamed of flight, while
we lie cozy in the bed in the little
white room with sloping ceilings
   in Mendocino.

Joanne Wilson,
from "the Summer of Love"

Marriage

Marriage is not dollars and dimes
Not beauty that is skin deep
But
Two hearts joined together
Holding hands
Journeying
Through
Sunny days
And
Stormy nights
With
Gratitude
In their hearts
Knowing
They are journeying
Together
On
This planet
Called Earth
Even
For a twinkling
Of an eye.

Hi-Dong Chai

Fifty Years[11]

An anniversary
"biography"
culled
during
eventful
fifty,
giving
highlighted
interests (of)
Joe (&)
Kathy:
loving
many
noisy
offspring;
playing & partying;
revisiting
quad (of)
Stanford;
traveling together;
uncoupled
volunteering;
wonder-filled
xhilarating
years.
Zowie

Kathy Cusick

She Smiled

They sat quietly in the corner,
In a sunset glow . . .
Of light and love and sadness.
He took her hand,
And, she smiled with her eyes,
And he with his mouth.
The sight of them together,
Softened my soul.
Life is precious,
As is love . . .
And, both are fragile.

Roberta Bondelie
(2016)

Poems for Guys

The Old Bar
Longfellow's Wayside Inn
Sudbury, Massachusetts

Cigars & Beer[12]

Ahhh!, my beer,
Here,
A quid's worth,
With all its mirth,
I sip . . . with good cheer,
My beer.
Served upon this tavern's polished bar,
As I contemplate from afar,
Life's true pleasures,
Ahhhh, what treasurers,
A chestnut brown,
Served around.

Outside, a chill and mist,
No summer day with all its bliss,
But in this Village Wayside Inn,
Within,
Softly heard a crackling fire—
Flame and ember do conspire
To cast a flickering shadow dance . . .
That does entrance;
As I light this fine cigar,
And take a sip of my beer—no finer riches are,
Of bright good cheer—
Cigars & Beer.

Another think I,
As I spy,
A Guinness dark,
That'll make you bark,
Or perhaps an ale,
Amber 'n pale,
Or perhaps a stout,
That some would tout,
But no . . . a rich nut-brown,
Is what I've found,
To be my taste,
This winter's eve that has no haste.

Here I sit,
While old nostalgic memories flit,
Like circled smoke-wreaths from my cigar,
That pass and drift—near, then afar.
And then it's here!
My beer,
A pint no less,
A frothy draught poured at its best,
Another smoke from my cigar,
How fine I think these riches are,
Of right good cheer—
Cigars & Beer.

—*Michael Breuleux*—
    Fall 2011

Warning! The following limericks include off-color and bawdy language. To put these limericks in perspective, Gershon Legman (1917-1999) compiled a scholarly anthology about limericks (*The Limerick*, Paris: Les Hautes Etudes, 1953; New York: Bell Publishing Company, 1969; New York: Random House LLC, 1988) and held that the true limerick is a folk, literary form and is always risqué and bawdy, and sometimes crude. Legman cites similar opinions expressed by Arnold Bennett and George Bernard Shaw. In his anthology, Legman characterized the "clean" limerick as a "periodic fad and object of magazine contests, rarely rising above mediocrity." The classic limerick is written predominantly in five-line anapestic meter with a strict rhyme scheme of aabba.

Bark!

There was a gent named Maloney,

Who trashed a lot of baloney;

He said dogs would bark,

When he broke a fart;

So he farted just to show me.

Phlatus

There was once a young lad named Phlatus,

Who would never cease to amaze us.

He could light a fart—

It was quite an art,

For the flash was seen at ten paces.

McGee

There once was an old man named McGee,

Though tried did he—no dump would be;

So he went to the pot,

And reward was his lot—

A Gordian lump passed as he peed!

Barooon

There once was an ol' slob named Barooon,
You'd swear he was a wrinkled old prune;
A scented smell had he,
For he broke wind you see;
And oft' he missed the saloon's spittoon.

Grump

There once was a loser named Grump,
Who was a political chump;
His failed insurrection,
As was his erection,
Caused Grump the chump to take a dump.

Cheney

A strong woman named Cheney there was,
Who swore an oath to a sacred cause;
With chaos exploding,
She stood firm extolling,
"No one is above, the rule of law."

'9ers and Bucs

My leather recliner, like a friendly old shoe,
Rests my bod—makes me feel anew.
Feet propped up with the TV on,
Friends all around and it won't be long.

It's the '9ers and Bucs in a gladiator duel,
What we don't know: the '9ers—the fool.
Good friends have come to watch the game,
The Bucs scored? . . . Man!, that's lame.

Nachos are passed and brewskis too,
"Hey, girls! . . . watch that language, will you."
Coach Mooch paces up and down,
Damn! . . . that T.O.'s one big clown!

Our wideout's down on a double-reverse!
Oh, no! . . . there's nothing worse,
Our biggest threat's out for the day,
How can we stop Tampa Bay?

Garcia drops back—T.O. down the middle,
What! . . . holding? . . . that play was a fizzle.
Handoff to Hearst—he's stopped at the line,
No gain there—that's not a good sign.

It's the end of the game and the Bucs have won,
Won's not the word, the '9ers are done.
The Bucs looked good and won in a breeze,
Oh well, next year—"another brewski, please."

(A post-script to this playoff game,
Again a move that's very lame,
Owner York—in his ire,
Three days later—Mooch is fired.)

Honey Badger

Honey Badger's the '9ers' "D",
Honey Badger says, "You wait 'n see."

Honey Badger says, "We take what we please,"
Honey Badger says, "Look out! We comin' Brees."
Honey Badger says, "We don't need—
Honey Badger says, that cheap boun-teé!"
Honey Badger says, "We play with pride,"
Honey Badger says, "Pride be our guide."
Honey Badger knows, '9ers' two keys:
Honey Badger says, "You gotta have "D,"
Honey Badger says, "Smith gotta chuck hard,"
Honey Badger says, "If he don't . . . gonna be long ten yards."
Honey Badger says, "Red-Zone means, we score 6,"
Honey Badger says, "Red-Zone don't mean, 3-point kicks."

If Honey Badger wants the ball,
Well, Honey Badger takes the ball!

Honey Badger says, "Ya gotta risk it,
Honey Badger says, cause if ya don't, there ain't no biscuit!"
Honey Badger takes all it wants,
Honey Badger takes no taunts.
Honey Badger got three big 'iles:
Honey Badger's—mo-bile—a-gile—and—hos-tile.
Honey Badger says, "We hit hard."
Honey Badger says, "This ain't no Mardi Gras."
Honey Badger knows, Iron sharpens Iron,*
Honey Badger says, "Comp'tition gonna . . . bring us the crown."
Honey Badger says, "We see the Promise Land!"
Honey Badger says, "Super Bowl's lookin' grand!"

Honey Badger says, "You wait 'n see,"
Honey Badger's the '9ers' "D."

Proverbs 27:17a

Mike, a fan, NFL post-season 2012-2013

Capt'n Morgan & Wailer
(Morgan's Oath)

Morgan the captain—a brigand was he,
Capt'n Morgan the pirate who'd sailed the Caribe,*
He retired one day—to the Cay of Mount Gay—
The isle of his dreams that came true that day.
Off in the distance one balmy night—
Wailer his schooner on moorings lay
In the blue/black waters of Mount Gay Bay.
She was anchored taut with mast and spar
That crisscrossed the moon like a dungeon's bar.
'Twas a blue/black sky with diamond'd lights,
When Capt'n stopped on the beach that night,
He hoisted a tankard with full moon bright,
And *Wailer* swayed—off in the moonlight.

"To the good ship, *Wailer*, I've no dismay,
I've stood for myself and done it my way,
She's the rock of my life, I've no regrets,
To hell with the laggards and their damned bets!"
And off in the distance—*Wailer* swayed.
"Black Mark the dullards and thems who forget!

No quarter given; to hell with their threats!"
And *Wailer's* silhouette in the tide—
Her rippled reflection magnified.
"Whether foe or friend, they've all had their say,
Some I have known and then they've betrayed,
As a phoenix risen, their doubts I've belayed,
And I've wanted it thus to this very day."

Capt'n lifted his tankard—Zacapa he drank,
And off in the moonlight—*Wailer* swayed.

for Pete, my brother, on his birthday, April 2010
*Careeb (Caribbean Sea)

Silly Stuff

Mary
Company Halloween Party
Cardiometrics, Inc.
Mountain View, CA
1987

Froggie, Froggie[13]

Froggie, Froggie,
In a towel,

Froggie, Froggie,
With a scowl,

Froggie, Froggie,
Hear him shout,

Froggie, Froggie,
"Let me out!"

Froggie, Froggie,
Hits the ground,

Froggie, Froggie,
Hops around,

Froggie, Froggie,
"Let me be!

Froggie, Froggie,
You will see,"

Froggie, Froggie,
Turns around,

Froggie, Froggie,
Bends way down,

Froggie, Froggie,
Makes a sound,

Froggie, Froggie,
"You hear that?"

Froggie, Froggie,
Tips his hat,

Froggie, Froggie,
"See ya later,

Froggie, Froggie,
Later, gator."

Bet & Mike
May 2010

Cookie, Cookie[13]

Cookie, cookie
Can't fool me.

Cookie, cookie
Let me see.

Cookie, cookie
Chocolate bar.

Cookie, cookie
Can't be far.

Cookie, cookie
So well hidden.

Cookie, cookie
Just a smidgen?

Cookie, cookie
Chocolate chip.

Cookie, cookie
I'll take a nip.

Cookie, cookie
Lookie, lookie.

Cookie, cookie
One more cookie.

Cookie, cookie
In my tummy.

Cookie, cookie
Yummy, yummy.

Cookie, cookie
No more here.

Cookie, cookie
Shed a tear.

Bet & Mike
March 2007

Rub-a-dub-dub

Rub-a-dub-dub,
Wash your hands in the tub,
But not to the nub,
POTUS tells us.

This coronavirus,
It's not so desirous?
It's fake news among us!
Alternative facts: Just a cough 'n a cold, don't you see!

It's all a lie,
There's pie in the sky,
But they still make you cry—
It's all a conspiracy!

Wash your hands if you will,
But don't be a pill—
Just chill on the hill,
People love me—just trust me.

So cough in the can,
Then wash your hands—
But know it's a sham,
Says POTUS.

95032[14]

Here come ol' flat-top—groovin' to a *Big Bop*.
Cheap sunglass, takin' no sass,
Big Schmoo, kangaroo, Yahoo, lookieloo, cow's moo, boohoo—but,
He got *buuuuuggh*—
Toe-jam football.

23059[14]

Joojoo baseball.
He know you,
You know him; when he turn, he got slim.
Foot-in-the-tank, pedal to the metal;
There go ol' flat-top—groovin' to a *Big Bop*.

Tink and Hook

"Good evening, Tink," came the whispered voice.
He had a pointed hook and a saber too,
And a moustache drooped his nose.
A dominate stare he had for her, as he glanced about in a nervous way.
On a galleon's deck she stood—
And with a curious tone, she asked,
"Good evening, Hook, and how have you been?
I hope you are well this day."
His stare never left as he studied her there—
And he moved quickly about the deck.
A quizzical look came upon his face and a demand now he made.
"And where have you been my little one,
Where have you been?", asked he.
To this she answered thus:
"The Never Bird guided me here,
Guided me through Neverland Wood and then to Mermaid's Lagoon."
"And what news have you?" he asked,
"Of Peter Pan—of that damn Pan!—the Wonder Boy of Neverland."
And to this she answered thus:
"He's spending time with that Wendy, you know.
And my heart aches so when I know they're alone.
My heart aches so," she said.

His hook reached out and it graced her cheek,
and he smiled and continued to stare,
"Then we're alone. We're together tonight,
never fret my pet . . . my Tinkerbell,
you're with a man and not a boy, this I can guarantee."
Then off in the distance a dreaded sound—a dreaded sound he heard.
"Gulp!", he gasped and then he croaked,
"'Tis a tick-tock-croc! . . . or a croc-tick-tock?"
As his moustache twitched his nose.
A jittery look came upon his face and his eyes widened indeed.
"No matter," he said . . . "'tis all the same!
Pardon me Tink, but I must flee!"

Duck vs. *Tree*[15]

(a poetry slam-down)

There once was a Tree
Who thought he was free
To play against a Duck.

But sad to say,
Upon that day
The Tree really did suck.

"It wasn't fair.
I hurt my knee,"
The Tree was heard to say.

But the Mighty Duck of OR,
Kept running up the score,
And that's how it went all day.

But the Tree stood tall,
As he took the ball,
And rallied to the cause.

At the end of the game,
It wasn't the same . . .
A "Shakespearean end" it was.

The Tree roared back,
And the Duck went "quack,"
As the Tree scored at will.

(Ending No. 1)
Though foreshadowed doom,
There was no gloom,
As the Tree went to his two-minute drill.

(Ending No. 2)
Though foreshadowed doom,
There was no gloom,
For the Tree—the Duck did kill.

(There. That's much better. A slight improvement on the last line of our poem. It's so nice collaborating with you. K)

Ken Henry and Mike Breuleux
November 2012

Nosey Mouse

by Mayme "Mimi" Frommeyer[16]

Fun Fair for the Forest Friends

(a Nosey Mouse Story)
by Mayme "Mimi" Frommeyer

October is a beautiful month, especially in the forest. Nosey Mouse came out of the mouse house down near the old barn. He stood looking for his friends. Not one was in sight. He felt lonesome. At that moment his brother, Nippy, came humming down the path. He had been visiting the Forest Fairies who lived in the Tree House in the Big Oak Tree.

Nippy was excited and thrilled. "Oh Nosey," Nippy exclaimed, "the Fairies have a super idea! They think it would be fun to have a Fun Fair." Nosey and Nippy ran to tell their mother. Mam Ma Mouse said, "We, of course, will help." So away the two scampered to tell Mr. Owl, the squirrel family and all the Forest Friends. The Forest Friends liked the idea of having a Fun Fair, and all would pitch in to help. The Squirrel Family would bring nuts; the Rabbit Family would bring lettuce, carrots, and beans; and so it went. They also decided to invite their Barnyard Friends. The Pig Family said, "A Fun Fair will be fun!" They would plan the music for dancing and also bring sandwiches. The Goose Family said they would bring cakes and colored eggs. Then the fun and work began. Reddie Fox put up the merry-go-round. Hoppy Squirrel brought his teeter-totter board. The Pig Family set up the bandstand for the music. All the friends were busy, busy, busy! Old Mr. Owl was busiest of all. He was seeing that everything was in order. And at last, everything *was* in order!

Early next morning the Friends arrived at the Fun Fair. Reddie started the merry-go-round, and each Friend had a turn. Mr. Owl took tickets. The Pig Family struck up the music and they all danced: *Put your little foot . . . put your little foot . . . put your little foot right in.* Such fun! Time went by fast, but now it was time for lunch and all the goodies. In the distance the Friends heard *tinkle, tinkle, tinkle*. It was Bossy Cow coming down the lane, all dressed up with a pink bow on her tail. She was bringing milk for lunch.

After lunch there was more dancing. Goosey Lucy danced with Goosey Gander; Henny Penny danced with Cock-a-doodle; the Forest Fairies danced merrily about; each danced with their partner the square dance. Each Friend had one more ride on the merry-go-round and thanked Reddie for helping. He had made the day such fun. Then they all went to the Tree House to say, "Thanks" to the Forest Fairies for such a happy day.

Time to go home. *Swissssh*—here was Billy Breeze blowing Merrie Sunshine over the hill. She had been shining all day and enjoyed being part of the Fun Fair. Everyone had so much fun the Forest Friends decided to have a Fun Fair next year and invite even more Friends. Woody Woodpecker and Mr. Blue Jay had flown away for the weekend, but now, late in the day, they perched in the Big Oak Tree. They looked lonesome. So Mr. Owl flew up to them and said, "Next year we want our Feathered Friends to be part of our Forest Fun Fair."

~ *The End* ~

Mimi
Walnut Creek, CA
circa 1966

The Adventures of Ginger & Candy

(a Nosey Mouse Story)
by Mayme "Mimi" Frommeyer

Nosey Mouse went next-door to play with his kitty friends, Ginger and Candy. Since Mamma Kitty was not home, the three friends decided to have a little snitch of cheese. The cheese was so good, they decided to have some sausage with the cheese. Ginger, the little brown kitty, said, "Let's have some cookies too." But Candy, the little white kitty, said, "We have no cookies;" so the three friends had little snitches of maple sugar instead.

Mamma Kitty came home and when she saw Nosey Mouse snitching, she told Nosey to go right home and tell his mamma what he had done. Ginger and Candy thought it was funny to see their Mamma scolding Nosey; but when Mamma Kitty found out that Ginger and Candy had been snitching too, she told them how naughty it was and they had to stay in the house.

Candy and Ginger had to stay inside. Their mamma wouldn't let them go out in the yard. So they decided to get their mamma's yarn and play. Candy and Ginger ran after the ball of yarn. When the yarn got caught on the nightstand, Candy decided to do stunts. Ginger held the ball of yarn and Candy climbed up. Then they did all kinds of stunts. They turned summersaults, stood on their heads—but Candy liked climbing best. They looked outside and there were their friends having a good time. But Candy and Ginger liked playing inside with the yarn. Candy said, "Oh Ginger, look who is sitting on the patio cushion watching us." Candy and Ginger both looked out the window.

On the cushion sat three little girl kittens, Rosy, Posy and Cozy—all three had fat, friendly faces. They wanted to play with Ginger and Candy, but their mamma was taking them to a party. So they had to sit on the cushion until she was ready. When Candy and Ginger heard they were going to a party, they were sad because they wanted to go too. Ginger said, "Mamma, Rosy, Posy and Cozy are going to a party and we would like to go." Their mamma said, "You have been such sweet kittens—but no more snitches when I am not home—so I will take you downtown and buy you an ice cream cone."

Ginger and Candy asked their mamma if they could invite two friends. So they invited their kitten friends, Buster and Dusty. Mamma Kitty was so proud to take her kittens with her. Ginger and Candy, and Buster and Dusty felt sorry they could not invite Nosey—but Nosey's mamma was not very proud of him because he went next door to his kitty friends' house and had snitches; but Nosey promised he would not do that again. All four kittens went downtown with Mamma Kitty and all had ice cream cones; and Buster and Dusty, and Ginger and Candy thanked Mamma Kitty.

Dusty then decided to go home, but Buster decided to stay and play for a while. Ginger and Candy and Buster were in the backyard when Mr. Pluto, a neighborhood friend who lived next door, looked over the fence. Buster said, "Hi, Mr. Pluto, do you want to play?" Mr. Pluto smiled and said, "Let me show you what Mrs. Pluto and I have. Would you like to come over to our house?" So Ginger, Candy and Buster ran down the cobblestone path and over to the next-door yard. They followed Mr. Pluto to the garage. Mr. Pluto walked very quietly and spoke very low. He said, "Come and I'll show you what Mrs. Pluto and I have." And there in the basket were four of the cutest little puppies; all four were looking at their mamma. The mamma's name was "Lucy." Lucy was standing and admiring her puppies. She loves them so very much and she was glad Ginger and Candy and Buster came to visit.

~ The End ~

Ginger & Candy

1

2

3

4

5

6

Holidays

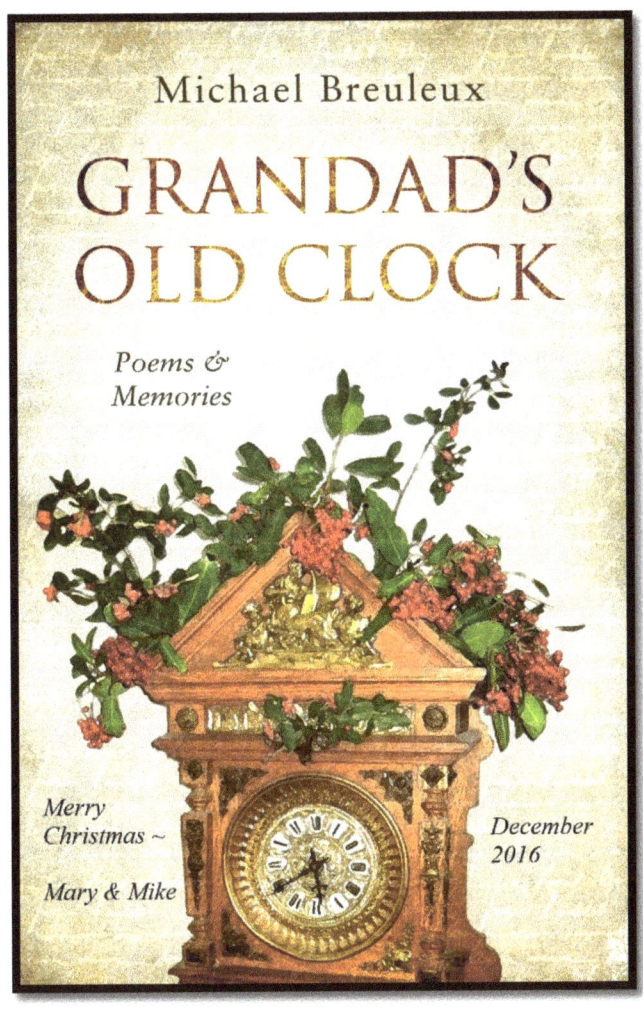

No Santa Claus![17]

There's a Santa Claus?
    There's faith and hope and love?
        Really?—
            "Balderdash!," I say.

"Santa's nothing but make-believe
    so kids would go to bed!",
        the Grinch who stole Christmas said without a pause.

I say, "Not so!"
    "There are no flying reindeer;
        there is no Merry Christmas family;
            there are no sugar-coated cookies
                for old Saint Nick."

"Tell mom and dad that
    faith and hope and love—
        and Santa
            are worth nothing but a lick."

No Santa Claus?[17]

Are worth nothing but a lick:
    Faith & Hope & Love
       & Santa.
           Tell Mom & Dad *that!*

For *Olde Saint Nick*—
    there are no sugar-coated cookies?
        there is no *Merry Christmas* family?
           there are no flying reindeer?
              I say, "Not so!"

The Grinch who stole Christmas said without a pause,
    "So kids would go to bed,
        Santa's nothing but make-believe."
           "Balderdash!," I say.

REALLY!
    There *is* Faith—& Hope—& Love—
        There *is* a Santa Claus!

Mary & Mike
Christmas, 1996
San José, California

Snow Bound

(a Christmas Holiday)

A snow-bound Christmas this December day—
Lake Tahoe's Holiday with fam'ly and friends;
A Christmas Tree cut and brought all the way,
Through Sierra storm for this Holiday.

A Silvertip found in West Point's foothills,
Layered green branches—spread out and even—
Tanenbaum garland'd with ornaments filled,
And "undertree" Village with country mill.

Cold walk thru the woods—in deepen'd, white snow[18]
To a pond frozen—enchant'd in stillness;
Currier & Ives that we'd surely know,
Of ice skating—bare oaks and mistletoe.

Our Tahoe cabin, warm-welcomes us all,
As clouds of snowflakes swirl in deep silence;
A yellow'd-red fire, sings brightly to all—
Yule log burns gaily thru shadow'd nightfall.

Everybody knows—some roasted turkey—
Pumpkin pie too—help make the Season bright;
Candles and *Spode* set the table early,
As a winter's snow caresses lightly.

Old Dad's Christmas Nog—poured slow with rum-spice,
Nog & Nutmeg—served to cheers and smiles bright!
A taste of fruitcake (but only a slice),
Pigmania! say all—Let's roll the pig-dice!

Good laughter abounds with jolly good fun,
As chestnuts roast on a warm, open fire;
A snouter Lyle rolls!—he's on a good run,
Leaning jowler then too!—he's far from done!

A snow-bound Christmas this December day—
With family and friends is our desire
To wish Merry Christmas—for all to say,
Happy Christmas to all this Holiday.

Michael Breuleux, 2022

Christmastide Angel

A Ω

~

*A*dvent's
*N*atal holy star,
*G*lories stream on high,
*E*arth receives His peace and
*L*ove for all humankind He gives.

*A*ngel,
*N*octurnal journeyer,
*G*ilding the passageways of Time,
*E*mmanuel, foretold by Your prophets old,
*L*ord, lift up thy holy messenger; herald the Messiah born.

*A*nointed One,
*N*ight of thy holy birth,
*G*od in Christ to earth descended,
*E*ternal flame that lights our darkest void,
*L*ight of light, hope of hope, You transcend our mortal world,

O Christ.

~ Angel ~
Tile detail of frieze on the staircase that ascends
to the chapel of *Nossa Senhora dos Remédios*
Lamego, Portugal
Photograph by Alice Bailey
2017

pax in terra et beneuolentia in hominibus

Christmas Peace

The anger of War erupts across the Ukraine,
as the rage of Evil sweeps in from the East.
Children—
hold their mothers' hands and trudge westward,
away from the thundering bombs, the strike of missiles
and the bomb-laden drones.
Snow falls and their bear-eared hoodies bob in the wind.
"Protected" by their teddy bears and *Raggedy Ann's*,
children struggle to the West and safety.
A little girl bends down and clutches her blanket . . .
kneels . . . huddles . . . and hides her face,
exhausted . . . scared . . . and afraid.
    Such is the madness of War.

Insurrection pounds on our Capitol's door
as the ghosts of Nuremberg and the Rallies
stream on our computers and TV's—and into our homes;
On the horizon, the *Doom of Democracy* marches.
Lies, asinine conspiracy theories and violent hate
rage through our political landscape—
Truth and civility are no more.

It is break-ins and hammers and broken knees
that now define our social discourse.

> What are we becoming?
> or—
> have become.

But then for a moment, some of us stop—(and pray all would stop);
And we hear and feel—the Silence—
Peace!
It is, as Maya reminds us—the Glad Season,*
But there is more—
It is the Season of our living Hope,
for today we celebrate the Peace, the Love,
the Joy, the undeserved Forgiveness
of Immanuel—of the Anointed One—of Jesus Christ.
Peace!
It is a Peace—not just the absence of War and Insurrection
and broken knees—
it is the Peace of the perfect Shalom of Christ;
For today Christmas comes to bring:
> Peace & Goodwill among men;
> Peace & Goodwill among women;
> Peace & Goodwill among earth's humanity.

---

*   Maya Angelou, *Amazing Peace, A Christmas Poem* (New York: Random House, 2005), verse 5, line 1.

Looking at a Ringed Moon on New Year's Eve[19]

What yonder moon shines crystal bright,
On this frosty December night?
Midnight's wonder this New Year's Eve,
Our party marvels at the sight.

We look again—our eyes deceived?
A circled moon—would you believe!
A bright thin ring of silver'd thread,
Rings the moon like a lacey weave.

Is this a sign of what's ahead,
As this Old Year is put to bed?
New Year's good tidings do portend,
As bold new prophets now have said?

So ring in the New, O good friends,
The Old is out—we're on the mend!
To do good works by New Year's end,
To do good works by New Year's end.

for Lizanne & Fred
January 1, 2010

for Mary

> Pupil: **Mary Melanson**   Grade: **5**
>
> FOURTH REPORT PERIOD
>
> Dear Mary,
>
> You have the wonderful ability to look life right smack in the eye and not back up a foot! You have lots of courage. Yours is the pioneer spirit. Never lose this ability Mary, as life will never defeat you. Remember to be gentle with others as all do not have your toughness of spirit. Also remember to accept love that people offer you for this is the secret of happiness.
>
> Love,
> Annabel Black — Parent

Progress report of Mary Melanson

Grade 5, June 15, 1956

Ms. Annabel Black, teacher

Endnote No. 20

I Understood

I met a princess in a dream,
She was kind and touched my hand,
"A gift I bring,"—she spoke serene,
Her soul so deep—her peace so grand;
And I wondered of her gift to me,
I wondered what her gift would be.

Side by side we walked that morn,
Through blissful meadow—through enchanted wood,
We walked and talked as the sun shone warm;
O, how I felt her peace—and sainthood.
And I began to understand,
And I began to understand.

Through a wood we did walk—
A lovely wood it was—
Out of the wood we emerged onto a boulder'd rock
That overlooked wave and beach—that gave me pause;
And then I understood,
And then I understood.

Michael Breuleux

Everything

You are everything to me,
You are everything through joy and strife,
You are the center of my soul,
You are the center of my life,
You are everything, my love,
You are my everything—you are my wife.

for Mary on your birthday
from Michael, your husband
June 2012

The Rose

Tho' the snows of winter
Will come into our lives,
And the two of us no more
In this mortal place—
Know there is no end to
The love of you and me,
No end to the love we share,
For I will meet you with a rose—*a kiss;*
And hand in hand, we'll forever be.

for Mary from your husband,
February 2007

I Wondered as I Wandered

I wondered as I wandered how her life will be,
Of what I see and do not see,
And how such things will come to be.

I wandered as I pondered all she means to me,
Of her love and spirit—and her intimacy,
Of her tears and smiles—and how I love her free.

I wondered as I wandered how her life will be,
If God so hears the sparrow and the roaring sea,
God must hear my prayer for her, prayed on bended knee.

for Mary
June 26, 2016
by Michael Breuleux

The Book Club
Seated left to right: Mary Breuleux, Lizanne Oliver
Standing left to right: Sandi Lococo, Jenefer Curtis, Alice Bailey
July 17, 2015

Mary's Song[21]

Yesterday you were with me still,
Your laugh, your smile, your strength, your will,
You fought the long and gallant fight,
Today, O empty day, you're gone,
And my heart sings but an empty song.

I'll miss you, Mary—my love, my wife,
I'll miss the spirit of your life,
I'll miss the little things you did so well,
I'll miss your touch and lingering spell,
I'll miss how we shared the song of life.

As your life's journey now does end,
I see you lifted as Jesus sends,
In His arms and for me you wait,
As God's host of angels gives you rest,
And Heaven's Song anoints you blest.

On the morrow waits eternity,
O'er Heaven's heights I'll search for thee,
I'll hear your voice on Heaven's high,
"Together now our love to keep,"
As a song sung with echoes deep.

The song within our hearts resounds,
A song of joy that has no bounds,
As does the love light in our eyes—
Like a thousand stars magnified,
And together we'll sing a song of love.

How sweet the song that we will sing,
Of waves and beaches and other things,
But the sweetest song that we will sing—
The sweetest song is yet to be—
Is the love we share for eternity.

for Mary Elizabeth Breuleux,
from your husband, Michael Breuleux
January 28, 2017

Stengel Beach at Sea Ranch, California's Mendocino Coast

12" x 18" acrylic
Lynden Keith Johnson
2017

Commissioned by
Mike Breuleux

In Memory of
Mary Elizabeth Breuleux
1945–2016

Reflections on a Himalayan Urn[22]

'tis alabaster of tinted rose and pale translucent light?
No, but lookest just as fair,
Thy silent shape soothes indeed—a pleasure to the sight;
How smooth and cool and softly radiant
Is thy pale, translucent shape;
Not of marble, not of stone, nor of painted clay,
But of Earth's ancient *salis* formed on a rocky mount.
Art thou but a fragile vessel placed in an ebb-tide sea?
Or doth thou hold eternal Truth?—
Doth the eons speak thru thee?

No leaf-fring'd legend—no flowery tale
Haunts about thy shape,
No pipers pipe, no timbrels play thru wood or dale
Doth thou portray;
But a simple Beauty is all thou hast.[22a]
O simple, simple Beauty!
If Truth is Beauty—
And Beauty—Truth (and that is all),
Then eternal Truth thou hast
Reflected by her Spirit and her Soul.

What lovely part thou did play in search
Of deep communion with the Saints
As Communion taken and Holy Spirit reached:
With bread and cup—
With prayer and grace,
Holiness was felt;
With bread broken—with wine poured
She came softly to ocean's reach;
And with His Love and with His Peace,
Her Spirit traced across the rocky beach.

O simple Beauty thou hast shown,
Yet deeper is thy Truth,
For by her Spirit, Truth I've known.
If no pipes are seen or heard,
If no timbrels are displayed,
Know that Heaven played its pipes and timbrels—
And played more yet for Heaven's HOST to hear;
As I bid my last goodbye to her—on that day—
Yet not goodbye in Time—
And released her to the Deep, as softly she slipped away.

Endnote No. 23

Parsley, Sage, Rosemary & Thyme

Though you are gone—
Your voice no more I hear,
Though my thoughts may wander far and near,
My love for you remains forever strong.

As I whispered my last good-bye (but not the last in Time),
Memories of you and yesteryear and the poet's rhythmic rhyme:
"Parsley, sage, rosemary and thyme"[24]
And your love I felt—the true love of mine.

Though you are gone—
Your touch no more I feel,
Your love does touch my heart to heal,
And our love remains as morning's dawn.

Stone Church Sanctuary
Sunday afternoon
May 8, 2017

Living Water

John 4:10
Numbers 20:1-13
1 Corinthians 10:4
Colossians 2:13-14

Living Water of Eternal Life
Wash away our sinful strife,
Wash away our many tears.
For the cross you will bear,
T'ward the hill of infamy,
T'ward desertion and despair.
Forty days your wearied journey—
Can't your suffering pain be spared?
O to know Your triumphant end—
For thirst we have of Living Water.
From the cross you will ascend—
Proclaim'd of GOD's imprimatur.
Hear us Water of Eternal Life!
From the Rock You've cleansed our strife.

Michael Breuleux
Lent, 2017

Living Water

(a sonnet)

John 4:10
Numbers 20:1-13
1 Corinthians 10:4
Colossians 2:13-14

O Living Water—path of righteousness,
You heard my plea to wash my sorrow'd tears;
LORD grant my prayer—forgive my sinfulness.
The Son of Man, my sin I saw you bear

Upon the cross—the cross of Calvary;
Desertion and disciples' sad despair,
You trod the path of lonely agony;
Cannot Your suffering torment be spar'd?

Then death You conquer'd—death You did transcend,
Your undeserv'd forgiveness cleans'd my debts,
As from the tortured cross You did ascend,
Devine anointment given—GOD did bless.

O Living Water from the Rock of Life,
Hosanna LORD!—you've healed my sinful strife.

I AM . . .

Mother, Father—Ima, Abba,
Creator of this earthly planet,
Hear my prayer,
Touch my heart,
Guide me in the way of Your righteousness.

—the Great Spirit,
Creator of the wind, the water, the fire and air,
Let me smell the sweet fragrance
Of the flowers that grace Your fields
That brings me closer to the Shepherd—my refuge.

Alpha & Omega,
Creator of the Universe,
Let me feel
The essence of Your energy,
To know the fire of Your presence.

The Beginning—the Light—the Source,
Creator of the Cosmic Silence,
Touch my existence,
Transform me,
Unite me with the groaning of Your Creation.

I AM—the Word,
Creator of Time and before-Time,
Enable my soul—
My being
To know You.

YHWH of old,
Creator of eternal truth,
Let me taste,
The sweetness of Your love,
Empower me through Your will to serve the tired and weak.

Abba, Ima—Father, Mother,
Creator of Wisdom;
Through the naked veil of my faults and sins,
Forgive me;
Grant that I may begin to know Your shrouded Mystery.

Father—

We thank You for the night,

And for the morning light,

For food and loving care,

And all that makes the world so fair.

Amen.

Rebecca J. Weston[25]
1885

Christ Washing the Feet of the Apostles
Meister des Hausbuches, 1475

O Love!

John 13:1-17, 31b-35, 15:12-13

"Now before the feast of the Passover, when Jesus knew that his hour had come to depart out of this world to the Father, having loved his own who were in the world, he loved them to the end. And during supper . . ."

Jesus, O Jesus, your earthly work draws nigh,
The feast has been prepared for you,
The feast—a holy rite.
You've heard the bell that tolls for thee,
Your disciples know not why,
A final lesson you will give,
So those who follow may love and live.

Rabbi, O Rabbi, you washed their feet that night,
Water from the upper room you took,
With girded towel on bended knee
The twelve you washed—disciples one by one
A humble task—but a sacred rite
Of unconditional love—*O Love!*—our Jesus!
The Son of man, forever near to us.

Lord, O Lord, leave us not we plead,
You answer thus, "O little children,
A new commandment to you I give:
Love one another; just as I have loved you.
My love for you is deep indeed,
For only love—*O Love!*—expressed with humbled heart,
Can bring this world eternal peace and bind your yearning hearts."

—Michael Breuleux
Maundy Thursday, 2012

The Shepherd's Prayer[26]

(Shepherd's prayer . . .
   Shepherd's prayer . . .)

The Lord is my Shepherd,
   I shall not want.

You make me lie down in green pastures
   and lead me beside still, quiet waters;
You, Lord, restore my soul.

You lead me on right paths for your name's sake.

   (so that I would remember You . . .
      so that I would live for Your reputation . . .)

Paths that are:
   noble,
   and true,
   and just,
   and pure.

Paths that are:
> caring
> and kind,
> and giving,
> and gracious.

For these are the paths that are pleasing to God;
For these are the paths that are praiseworthy of God;
These are the paths I will follow today as You, Jesus, lead me.

Even though I walk through the *Shadowed Valley of Death*,
> as I walk the path that Mary bravely walked before me,
> I fear no evil,
> for You, Lord, are with me,
> Your rod and Your staff
> They comfort me.

> *(they comfort me . . .)*

You prepare a table before me in the presence of my enemies;
> You prepare a warrior's homecoming banquet—
> my enemies are bound and defeated—
> my enemies are stripped of their power—
> my enemies threaten me no more;
> You, Lord, have defeated my enemies.

You anoint my head with oil
> and mantle me a brave warrior.

Michael Breuleux

My cup I hold—
>   the cup Mary and I together held—
>   overflows . . . and Your goodness and mercy and love flow forth;
>   my cup overflows with Your peace—
>   Your amazing grace—
>   Your undeserved forgiveness—
>   Your healing presence.

Surely all will follow me for the rest of my days;
>   all of which I thank You so much,
>   for all things come but from You, Lord;
>   and my days will come to an end . . . for surely they will.

I will then be . . .
>   a new creation—
>   a new being—
>   a new spirit—
>   in a higher realm of Your Kingdom—
>   >   where Your Peace reigns,
>   >   where Your Glory reigns,
>   >   where Your Majesty reigns,
>   >   where Your Power reigns.

Where two are as one—
>   where Mary and I will live . . . will be . . .
>   >   in the *House of the Lord*
>   >   forever—and ever—and ever,
>   >   for eternity—
>   >   Amen.

You Restore My Soul[27]

You make me lie down in green pastures
>and lead me beside still, quiet waters;
You, Lord, restore my soul.

You walk with me through *Sea Ranch* meadows and along
>the crooked *Bluff Trail* as it meanders beside the sea;
You stand with me on the cobbled sands of *Stengel Beach*
>as sea hawks and gulls wheel high above me;
Lord, You restore my soul.

You lead me along the old dirt road of *Sierra Azul*
>and show me *Tuscan* vistas;
On the warm, summer sands of *Capitola Beach* You are with me
>as I hear the ocean's waves roll to shore;[27]
You, Lord, restore my soul.

You are with me in the waters off *Monastery Beach* and on the great
>rift wall of *Monterey Canyon* as the deep silence calls;
You show me the *mola mola* that glides languid thru kelp'd, green
>waters as a *California moray* eyes me suspiciously from below;
Lord, You restore my soul.

You stand with me as I wait for the invitation to hike
    the trails of *Sierra Azul;*
You are with us on a chilly autumn day in the *Old Bar* of *Longfellow's*
    Wayside Inn as we share the afternoon next to a crackling fire;
You, Lord, restore our souls.

You greet us with a *skinny moon* over *Timber Cove*
    to celebrate our *Northern California* honeymoon as
    Bene Bufano's *Peace Sculpture* looms high;
You walk with us thru the narrow lanes and backstreets of *Mendocino*
    and show us the *serigraphs* of William Zacha;
Lord, You restore our souls.

You paint a *Caribbean* sunset of blue and gold and orange before our
    eyes as we dance on the beach to the rhythms of
    No Woman, No Cry;
On a cold Alpine ski slope, You are there as a gusty wind swirls
    white and blue and pink and green ice crystals around me;
You, Lord, restore my soul.

You lead me along the paths of *Montgomery Hill* and show me
    the blue *Ithuriel's Spear* and the *Scarlet Pimpernel;*
You sit with me in the shade of the *Oaks of Mamre*
    as eastward I look to the green and gold foothills beyond;
Lord, You restore my soul.

Over jagged *Sierra* peaks you hike with me
    as the *High Nevada Desert* beckons eastward;
You are with me on the rocky shores of *Angora Lakes*
    as I swim its icy waters;
You, Lord, restore my soul.

You walk with me at tide's edge along *Shell Beach*
    as the nightly waters reflect a ghostly moon;
You show me the meteors that trace Your heavens
    as the diamonded sky lights Your *Creation;*
Lord, You restore my soul.

You bring me peace amid the worldly chaos
    and hope among the ungodly;
You, Lord, restore my soul.

Michael Breuleux

The Vineyard[28]

(a one-act poem in four scenes)

Springtime Vineyard

Oh, what a glorious morning it was!
Working in the vineyard,
Tending vine and spading soil.
Butterflies dance and birds chirp,
Twisted vine and musty humus—
Springtime sights, sounds, smells and stirrings fill the vineyard!
Mother Sun warms the earth and stirs the dormant vine.
Life's force—coaxed from the soil—
Moves up to the furthest tip of last year's growth.
Make a pruning cut and see the vine's sap flow;
Let it drip on your tongue,
And discover its shy sweetness.
The vines sleep now,
But at the right moment, they'll awake,
And then—like giddy children—
They'll leap out and yell, "Boo!" to the world.

April 2005

Summertime's Vineyard

The old-vine vineyard heated by the sun,
'Neath a summer sky with clouds towered high,
Where dry, musty soil breathes a rich, warm scent,
And gray ground squirrels, quickly scamper and run.

A vineyard of old 'neath a warm blue sky,
Chard's pale green pearls on vines twisted and bent,
Where zin's purple grapes shimmer in the sun,
And a red-tailed hawk circles ever so high.

The old-vine vineyard—how magnificent,
A light summer breeze blows trellis and vine,
Where cab and merlot hide 'mongst leafy boughs,
And butterflies float o'er vines leaved and bent.

A vineyard of old whence comes the wine,
Where a creek bed meanders 'cross field and farm—
Across vineyard's way and toward an old mill pond,
And birds chirp and sing a song of summertime.

The old-vine vineyard where bees buzz and swarm,
Of cab and clear chard; of merlot and red zin;
Come autumn and harvest and cool fall days,
But now the summertime vineyard, lingers lazy and warm.

July 2011

Claire's Field in Autumn

Vineyard! O vineyard, where the grapes are there to grow,
On this morn the vineyard wakes, for today comes the harvest,
Of ripened chard, of purple zin—of cab and rich merlot,
Grapes clustered on trellis-quad, ready for the harvest.
    Leav'd in crimson, gold, and red-brick brown,
      the vineyard arrays autumn's gown;
      An autumn chill fills the air,
      O the harvest would be so fair.

Claire idles through vineyard rows and surveys her domain;
From leafy boughs hang the grapes ready for the picking;
Harvest not the cab and chard in twain, nor merlot and zin the same,
For today pick the ripened chard that awaits for the picking;
    Claire's soulful eyes search the keep,
      for gray ground squirrels in vineyard's deep;
      She does not see as once before,
      but a pat of love does she adore.

Wisps of smoke from a wood-fire distant, curl to a crisp, blue sky,
And above the vineyard in its array, a red-tailed hawk circles higher,
O harvest day of blue, fall skies and fluffy clouds that scuttle by,
Would the harvest be so grand even herald by Heaven's choir.

October 2014

Winter Vineyard

Bare twisted vines pruned and bent,
Silhouette a gray winter's sky,
Chilly cold days Jack Frost has sent,
To frost the vines on trellis lie.

Winter rye spreads a rich green carpet,
'Tween row and trellis—a wonderment,
Dewdrops clothe the rye grass wet,
And breathe the earth a crisp, clean scent.

We walk the vineyard with glass in hand,
A rich merlot of *Thomas Kruse*,
And feel the richness of the land,
Of vine and rye and frosty dew.

Deep sleep gray vines this winter's day,
Gnarled and pruned in vineyard's deep,
Await they do for spring's array,
For now they take their winter's sleep.

April 2014

Peace or *The Expanding Universe*
Sculptor: Beniamino "Bene" Bufano (1890-1970)
in collaboration with Alfonso Pardiñas of Byzantine Mosaics,
located on California's Sonoma Coast overlooking the Pacific,
approximately eighteen miles south of Sea Ranch.

On Sea Ranch

"I wanted to plan a unique community based on ecological principles of design and immersed in nature. We have an important responsibility here. What do we bring to this environment and how do we alter it? In some profound sense I feel myself a custodian rather than an owner. To this place which enriches my life, I feel I owe constant vigilance and care for its poetic and spiritual survival. I hope those who follow me feel the same."

Lawrence Halprin
Founding landscape architect
Sea Ranch, California
1964
(inscription on the entrance to
Black Point Beach, Sea Ranch)

I don't hike the trail until I'm invited.

Ken had returned to Stone Church after attending a pastors' retreat, the general theme of which was "Hiking and Spirituality." Upon his return, Ken, in one of his sermons, noted he was impressed with the retreat leader (an avid hiker like Ken), who made the point she never stepped on the trail until she was invited; by which she meant, she would stand at the trailhead and wait until the trail, the wilderness, the mountain or desert invited her. The invitation might come from a leaf that falls or a butterfly that floats across the trail; or a bird that sings or a clap of thunder; or something else. You'll know the invitation when you hear it or see it or feel it or even smell it. You may wait thirty seconds or you may wait five minutes, but you don't start to hike until you're invited. I've taken Ken's (and the retreat leader's) advice and now I don't just charge up the trail. I wait to be invited. After all, I am but a visitor.

Mike Breuleux
We'll miss you Ken and Heather.
2016

On the Kingdom of God, an Open Bible and My Dad[29]

Michael Breuleux, 1996

I do not know what the future Kingdom of God will be like. I do not know whether the "holy city, new Jerusalem" will come down out of heaven (Rev 21:2)*; or how God and the Lamb will "reign for ever and ever" (Rev 22:5); or how a "new heaven and a new earth" will be established (Rev 21:1). But when Jesus was asked by the Pharisees when the Kingdom would come, he answered them in this way:

> The kingdom of God is not coming with signs to be observed; nor will they say, "Lo, here it is!" or "There!" For behold, the kingdom of God is in the midst of you (Luke 17:20-21).

I am beginning to understand that the Kingdom of God is already here and I have experienced it—even though briefly. For now, the Kingdom flashes before us only to fade away as if we are "looking through a glass darkly." And then, at some future moment, it unexpectedly reappears. For me, I experienced the Kingdom several years ago. This was my experience:

My dad died in the afternoon of Easter Sunday, 1985. Dad had gone to his bedroom for an afternoon nap. An hour or so later, I remember hearing my brother-in-law, Pat, shout as he ran toward the back of the house that Dad had "fallen." When we got to Dad's side, he was gone. Probably all of you can relate to the emotion that takes over in the immediate hours and days after the sudden death of someone you love. That emotion was felt by my family and me. The paramedics came and took Dad away, and then later that afternoon I went back to his room, where he had died. My intent was to straighten things up so Mom would not have to deal with it. When I returned to Mom and Dad's room, I found Dad's Bible open on the floor. It was obvious the last thing Dad had in his hand was his Bible. I remember picking up Dad's Bible and glancing at an open page in the book of Luke. I cannot tell you the specific chapter of Luke, but there was Dad's Bible in front of me—open.

Until that Easter in 1985, I had never seriously read the Bible. The earliest memory I have of attempting to read the Bible was when I was in the eighth grade. I told myself then I would read the Bible "at least once." I started immediately with Genesis 1:1—"In the beginning . . ."—and I got as far as Genesis 4 or 5. And then I quit. After Dad died, something happened. On the morning of April 16, nine days after Dad died, I was praying, and while I prayed, I opened a Bible I had used in my college freshman humanities class. For some reason I opened it to Luke 24. This is the Emmaus story, and this is what Luke said to me:

> And their eyes were opened and they recognized him; and he vanished out of their sight. They said to each other, *"Did not our hearts burn within us* while he talked to us on the road, *while he opened to us the scriptures?"* (Luke 24:31-32, emphasis added)

I have read the Bible ever since—most of the time rather slowly—and at times, I admit, sporadically. I started this time with Mark (probably because it is the shortest gospel) and after over eleven years, I have almost finished reading the Bible—"at least once." I wish I could say I understand Scripture, but I am beginning to have a better understanding of what the Bible is teaching me and how its message applies to my life. For me, the Kingdom of God touched my life ever so briefly that distant Easter afternoon and nine days thereafter, and for a moment I felt God's everlasting Kingdom.

* Scripture citations are from the Revised Standard Version.

Mary & Mike
Clear Lake, California
June 2012

Sunday, November 19, 2017

I had a dream about Mary last night. It wasn't really "nighttime"—more like early morning. I know because I heard Grandad's Old Clock strike 5:00 AM. Anyway, I went back to sleep a little after 5:00, I guess, and a dream about Mary came to me. It was a good dream. I dreamt we were in a house someplace. It was a fairly large house—but not exceptionally large—and there were outside stairs, painted white, that went from the lower backyard to the upstairs main floor—sort of like the Fribley's house in Walnut Creek that I knew as a kid. The house was on the side of a hill, and it seemed a very pleasant house. The backyard, where Mary and I were, was well landscaped with green shrubs around the perimeter, and there were some trees too. Nothing grand, but it was a pleasant place. There were a lot of people in the backyard with us. However, besides Mary, the only other person I was aware of was Susie, Mary's younger sister, who read "The Shepherd's Prayer" (Psalm 23) at Mary's memorial service. In my dream, it was known (*felt* is probably a better word) that Mary had been very ill and had a very hard time breathing (because of the emphysema and bronchiectasis from which she suffered). So Mary's condition *was* known and felt. But that was *not* Mary's condition in my dream, because Mary was radiant and healthy and alive.

I looked over at Mary, who was in front of me and to my right, but not too far away. She was sitting by herself, but still in the group, and at the edge of a green grass lawn. There were some green shrubs behind her, and Mary was wearing an off-white, beige-colored dress that appeared light and made perhaps of a fine cotton or linen material. It was a simple dress . . . nothing fancy. Just before this, Susie, for some reason, had handed me a hairbrush. The brush was made of something that appeared very clear, almost crystal-like, and inlaid with what appeared to be mother-of-pearl. I looked over at Mary and she looked at me; and then I walked over to her and bent down (because she was sitting on the lawn). We didn't say anything. We looked at each other, and Mary smiled at me and I at her, and then I knelt down and we took each other in our arms and hugged each other for what seemed like a long time. It was then I noticed Mary's hair. Her hair was radiant! It was bright and shiny and soft, and it had the most beautiful luster. Her hair had a sheen that was very soft and subtle. I noticed that Mary was wearing her hair a little longer, but not too much longer, than she usually did. And she looked beautiful. Then I dreamt I took the hairbrush Susie had given me, and I brushed Mary's hair. I just brushed her hair. Nothing special.

It was early evening, I guess, because I said I was going to dinner (in the main dining room at The Terraces, I suppose). Mary said she would like to go to dinner too because she felt good, but she would rather go another day. Then Mary and I got up and walked to the stairs (which I wrote about), and we climbed the stairs to the upper part of the house. When we walked up the stairs, a large group of people walked with us—but behind us. I remember I looked around, and Mary asked who I was looking for, and I said I was looking for Susie because I wanted to thank her for the hairbrush. And Mary said Susie was right behind me. So I turned and thanked Susie for the hairbrush, and then we walked outside—apparently out the front door of the house. We walked out to a nice neighborhood street. It seemed like early evening because it was getting dark, but the street had streetlights that were softly lighted, and there were nice bushes planted on both sides of the street, and there were some older trees too. It was not a very wide street, and it looked like the street went up a hill to the right, and to the left the street curved downhill slightly. We looked out at the street, and then my dream ended and I woke up.

It was a little before 7:00 in the morning, and I had wanted to get up earlier and read before I got ready for church. But that was okay. (This Sunday I went to the Presbyterian Church of Los Gatos with Jo Ann and Milt K., friends at The Terraces, because the stated clerk of the Presbyterian Church was preaching, and Jo Ann wanted me to hear him. I wasn't going to Stone Church this particular Sunday.) I have a spiritual sense this dream was a gift—a gift from Jesus the Christ. I don't know why it was given to me. This is the first dream I've had of Mary since she died the morning of December 27, 2016.

Godspeed

There is a feeling deep within me that can never let Mary go, but there is also the feeling that sends her on her way. This is a contradiction—to hold on and to let go at the same time—and I don't understand it. Nevertheless, it is there. It's one of the mysteries. So Mary—my wife, my love, my everything—as you leave, know I will catch up to you in Time's eternity.

Mike, your husband
from my Journal
Thursday, November 16, 2017

Endnotes

1. Don Blanding, *Joy Is an Inside Job* (New York: Dodd, Mead & Company, 1953, 1963).

2. Perry "P.C." Conner, in conversation.

3. The Sea Ranch is mentioned several times in my book. Sea Ranch is an architectural experiment that engages the land and sea with the wind, air, rain and sun. Geographically, Sea Ranch is located on California's northern Sonoma Coast. The small Mendocino County coastal town of Gualala approximates the boundary between Sonoma and Mendocino counties. More precisely, the Gualala River, just south of Gualala, forms the boundary between Sonoma County and Mendocino County before the river flows into the Pacific Ocean. Sea Ranch's northern border is about one mile south of the Gualala River Bridge. For whatever reason, I always referred (erroneously) to Sea Ranch being on California's Mendocino Coast—most probably because of the connection Mary and I had with the coastal art community of Mendocino located north of Sea Ranch. For an in-depth history and philosophy of Sea Ranch, see *The Sea Ranch, Fifty Years of Architecture, Landscape, Place, and Community on the Northern California Coast*, by Donlyn Lyndon and Jim Alinder, with essays by Donald Canty and Lawrence Halprin (New York: Princeton Architectural Press, 2004, 2014).

4. "Grandad's Old Clock," the following sources and notes are referenced:

Hebrew Scriptures: Gen 1:1-2:3, 4:26b, 17:1; Ex 3:13–15, 6:1–3; Lev 19:17, 34; Deut 6:4–9, 11:13–28; Job 28, 38–41; Ps 8, 19:1–6, 33:6–9, 104; Prov 3:5–8, 13–26, 8; Eccl 3:1–15; Isa 40:13–14, 44:6-8; Jer 29:13.

Apocrypha: Wis 6:12–23, 7:15–8:8, 8:21–9:4a, 9:9–11; Sir 1:1–20, 6:22, 6:26–31, 15:1, 18:1–14, 19:20, 24:1–22, 51:13–30; 2 Macc 7:28.

New Testament: Mt 6:9–15 (see the doxology based on David's prayer, 1 Chr 29:10-18), 22:34–40; Mk 12:28–34; Lk 10:25–37, 11:1–4; Jn 1:1–5; Rom 11:33–35; 1 Cor 13:12; Heb 11:1–3, 13:8; Jas 2:8–10; Rev 1:8.

The "family travel history" of Grandad's Old Clock is the following: Cincinnati, Ohio; Amory, Mississippi; Vicksburg, Mississippi; Memphis, Tennessee; Walnut Creek, California; San José, California; Los Gatos, California.

The "custodianship" of Grandad's Old Clock is the following:
- circa 1895: E. A. "Grandad" Frommeyer of Cincinnati, Ohio, won the Old Clock in a horse race (see entry below).
- 1940: Given to F. E. "Fritz" Breuleux on his engagement to Betty Rae Frommeyer (granddaughter of Grandad) of Cincinnati, Ohio.
- 1985: Given to Michael Breuleux of Los Gatos, California (son of Fritz Breuleux).
- Grandad's Old Clock will be given to Kyle Breuleux (nephew of Michael Breuleux).

Grandad always told the story how he won the Old Clock in a horse race. Mam Ma, Grandad's wife, however, told us Grandad's account was somewhat "embellished" and was not exactly how the Old Clock was acquired by the Frommeyer family. Personally, I prefer Grandad's story.

Julian Barbour, *The Janus Point, A New Theory of Time* (New York: Basic Books, 2020).

Kenny Barron (piano) and Buster Williams (base), *Two as One*, album recorded live at the Teatro Morlacchi, Perugia, Italy, 1986, Umbria Jazz Festival, released on the Italian Red label.

Albert Einstein, *Relativity, The Special and the General Theory* (New York: Wings Books, 1916, 1961 by the Estate of Albert Einstein). Thank you Rex Allen for introducing me to Einstein's book and for helping me understand, at a very basic level, Einstein's Special and General Theories.

Pallab Ghosh, "Stephen Hawking's final interview: A beautiful Universe," BBC News, Science, March 26, 2018; https://www.bbc.com/news/science-environment-43499024.

Thomas Gray (1716–1771), "Elegy Written in a Country Churchyard" influenced in part the structure of "Grandad's Old Clock."

4a. Stephen Hawking, *A Brief History of Time* (New York: Bantam Books, 1988, 1996, 2017). Hawking does not use the term "Unified Complete Theory of Everything," nor does he use the term "Theory of Everything" (T.O.E.). He does use the terms "unified theory" and "complete theory" (pp. 190, 191).

Chris Impey, *How It Began, A Time-Traveler's Guide to the Universe* (New York: W. W. Norton & Company, 2012).

Michio Kaku, *The God Equation, The Quest for a Theory of Everything* (New York: Doubleday, 2021). My thanks to James Dieterich for introducing me to Dr. Kaku's book.

Ben Keyes, "The Vineyard and the Vine: Reflections on the Biblical Theme of Winemaking," L'Abri Fellowship, Southborough, Massachusetts, Resources, February 21, 2020 lecture, especially at 1:08:00–1:15:45, https://southboroughlabri.org/.

4c. Lawrence M. Krauss, *A Universe from Nothing* (New York: Free Press, A Division of Simon & Schuster, Inc., 2012). "There are known knowns. These are things we know that we know. There are known unknowns. That is to say, there are things that we know we don't know. But there are also unknown unknowns. There are things we don't know we don't know" (Donald Rumsfelt, p. 23).

Lisa Rosenberg, *A Different Physics* (Santa Fe, New Mexico: Red Mountain Press, 2018); see especially the poems, "Introduction to Methods of Mathematical Physics" (p. 9) and "A Different Physics" (p. 69).

4b. Michio Kaku, Ph.D., Professor of Theoretical Physics, City University of New York, writes in his book, *The God Equation*:

"I find it utterly staggering that all the known laws of the physical universe can be summarized on a single sheet of paper.

Contained on the paper is Einstein's (general) theory of relativity. The Standard Model is more complicated, taking up most of the page with its zoo of subatomic particles. They (Einstein's general theory and the Standard Model) can describe everything in the known universe, from deep inside the proton to the very boundary of the visible universe.

Given the utter brevity of this sheet of paper, it is hard to avoid the conclusion that this was planned in advance, that its elegant design shows the hand of a cosmic designer. To me, this is the strongest argument for the existence of God" (Kaku, *supra*, p. 188).

As Dr. Kaku states, ". . . all the known laws of the physical universe can be summarized on a single sheet of paper." Einstein's General Theory of Relativity can be summarized in an equation about one and one-half inches long. This equation describes the first of the four fundamental Forces of Nature (i.e., Gravity):

$$G_{\mu\nu} \equiv R_{\mu\nu} - \frac{1}{2} R g_{\mu\nu} = \frac{8\pi G}{c^4} T_{\mu\nu}$$

The Standard Model equations (below in highly abbreviated form) require most of the page. The Standard Model details our quantum universe of thirty-six quarks and anti-quarks; electrons, neutrinos, protons, neutrons and gluons; twelve weakly interacting particles and anti-particles (called leptons); and a large assortment of Yang-Mills fields and Higgs bosons. The equations describe the relationship between the three remaining fundamental Forces of Nature (i.e., the Strong Nuclear Force, the Weak Nuclear Force, and the Electro/Magnetic Force):

$$\mathcal{L} = -\frac{1}{2} \text{Tr} G_{\mu\nu} G^{\mu\nu} - \frac{1}{2} \text{Tr} W_{\mu\nu} W^{\mu\nu} - \frac{1}{4} F_{\mu\nu} F^{\mu\nu}$$

$$+ (D_\mu \phi)^\dagger D^\mu \phi + \mu^2 \phi^\dagger \phi - \frac{1}{2} \lambda \left(\phi^\dagger \phi\right)^2$$

$$+ \sum_{f=1}^{3} (\bar{\ell}_L^f i \not{D} \ell_L^f + \bar{\ell}_R^f i \not{D} \ell_R^f + \bar{q}_L^f i \not{D} q_L^f + \bar{d}_R^f i \not{D} d_R^f + \bar{u}_R^f i \not{D} u_R^f)$$

$$- \sum_{f=1}^{3} y_\ell^f (\bar{\ell}_L^f \phi \ell_R^f + \bar{\ell}_R^f \phi^\dagger \ell_L^f)$$

$$- \sum_{f,g=1}^{3} \left(y_d^{fg} \bar{q}_L^f \phi d_R^g + (y_d^{fg})^* \bar{d}_R^g \phi^\dagger q_L^f + y_u^{fg} \bar{q}_L^f \tilde{\phi} u_R^g + (y_u^{fg})^* \bar{u}_R^g \tilde{\phi}^\dagger q_L^f \right)$$

As noted by Dr. Kaku, it is astonishing that all the physical laws of the Universe can be derived from this one, brief page of equations. (The above equations can be found in Kaku, *supra*, p. 208.) The "quest" of theoretical physicists is to combine the two theories and express them in "an equation whose mathematical elegance" encompass all the laws of the cosmos "starting from the Big Bang and moving to the end of the universe."

Author's Note: The equations set forth in Dr. Kaku's book do not "prove" that God exists and should not be taken as such. Rather, as Greg Cootsona notes in his book, *Mere Science and Christian Faith* (Downers Grove, IL: InterVarsity Press, 2018), they are "the fingerprint(s) of God" (p. 78). Cootsona continues, "This is not a deductive proof for God that leaves no room for disagreement. Instead it's a suppositional argument that offers confirmation … that this universe has design and that design is confirmed by the incredible particularity of its parameters" (*ibid.*, 79).

5. "Flight 93 (*the 40*)": This poem follows in part the structure of "Paul Revere's Ride" (1863) published in *Tales of a Wayside Inn* by Henry Wadsworth Longfellow (1807–1882). Historically, Paul Revere, William Dawes, and Samuel Prescott rode the night of April 18, 1775. A day later, Israel Bissell rode. Bissell rode to Philadelphia along the Old Post Road with news of the British attack on Lexington and Concord. It's reported he rode four days and six hours; his ride covered 345 miles from Watertown, Massachusetts, to Philadelphia. Two years later, on April 26, 1777, Sybil Ludington (age sixteen) made a similar ride. She rode in a rainstorm a total of forty miles, almost twice the distance Revere rode, to warn the local militia of an impending British march on Danbury, Connecticut where the Continental Army had a supply depot. Ludington was congratulated for her heroism by General Washington. The line "And fired the shot heard 'round the world" is quoted from "Concord Hymn" by Ralph Waldo Emerson (1803–1882).

5a. The passengers who directly led the "charge" and were involved in taking back control of the aircraft were: Todd Beamer, Mark Bingham, Flight Attendant Sandra Bradshaw, Thomas Burnett, Jeremy Glick, Louis Nacke, and Flight Attendant Deborah Welsh. Captain Jason Dahl was the pilot. For the list of passengers and crew on United Airlines Flight 93 see "Friends of Flight 93, National Memorial," www.flight93friends.org.

6. "A Chance Encounter": This poem was inspired in part by a late-afternoon ski run down Stagecoach, Heavenly Valley, Lake Tahoe. It had been a "bluebird day" with high, white clouds piled against a deep blue sky. The last ski run was before me; the sun was going down; I was alone on the mountain; and the late afternoon was getting cold. When I looked up the moguled ski run, a gusty wind picked up snowy ice crystals and created swirls of little white clouds across the mountainside. They looked like puffs of fluffy cotton being blown here and there. Then the wind shifted and came to me and tossed the crystals to the sun and a shower of white and blue and pink and green swirled around me. It was beautiful. Then it was over and I skied down the mountain. "Canadian Sunset" (1956, music by jazz pianist Eddie Heywood and lyrics by Norman Gimbel) also inspired this poem. The line "away from the madding crowd," is adapted from Thomas Gray's "Far from the madding crowd's ignoble strife" found in "Elegy Written in a Country Churchyard" (1751).

7. "Emma Rae": Emma Rae Dykhouse is my great-niece and the daughter of Jessie and Brad Dykhouse.

8. haiku: "mola mola", inspired by the sighting of a mola mola on a SCUBA dive trip with my brother, Pete, off Monastery Beach, south of Carmel; "monarch", inspired by Kendric Smith's monarch butterfly exhibits and displays at The Terraces of Los Gatos.

9. "Stephen Hawking tries to put God in a box": Read together, these two poems are a reverso poem, a poetry form invented by Marilyn Singer. If you read the first poem and then read the poem again with the lines reversed, with changes only in punctuation and capitalization, the two poems should say something completely different. A good friend, Lizanne Oliver, introduced me to the reverso poem.

10. "Ukraine's Children": My thanks to Susan Black Sweeting for her comments about "Ukraine's Children" and for recommending the 60 Minutes documentary, "Multinational effort working to save

kids with cancer in Ukraine." Susan's comments and the documentary helped me write "Ukraine's Children" the way I wanted it written. Thank you so much Susan. (The above documentary by Scott Pelley can be found at: https://www.cbsnews.com/news/ukraine-children-cancer-st-jude-hospital-convoy-of-life-60-minutes-transcript-2023-06-25/.)

11. "Fifty Years": This poem, written by a good friend, Kathy Cusick, is in the form of an alphabet poem. The poem was written for Kathy and Joe Cusick's fiftieth wedding anniversary, celebrated on 02/02/02. It was printed on Kathy and Joe's anniversary party invitation.

12. "Cigars & Beer": George Arnold (1834–1865) wrote a memorable poem entitled "Beer." The pattern, rhythm, and some phrases in Arnold's poem are reflected in my poem. Arnold's poem is somewhat melancholy and I wanted to write something a little more "cheery— of bright good cheer." The "beer" came from a chilly, autumn afternoon spent with Mary in The Old Bar of Longfellow's Wayside Inn, Sudbury, Massachusetts, where we talked and played cribbage next to a crackling fire that the bartender made for us. I drank a couple Samuel Adams beers, and Mary had her tea. The reference to "cigars" came from an aborted ski trip to Lake Tahoe with three friends and is another story. The "cigars" have nothing to do with Mary. Mary did not tolerate such smoke.

13. "Froggie, Froggie" and "Cookie, Cookie": written in collaboration with my sister, Betty Blote.

14. "95032" and "23059": These nonsense poems are in the form of a Zip Ode and a Reverse Zip Ode. A Zip Ode is a poem written in the format of your zip code (see a collaboration between WLRN and O, Miami, at https://www.wlrn.org/write-an-ode-to-your-zip-code). A good friend, Claudia Hamm, introduced me to the Zip Ode. The following sources are referenced: "You Can't Catch Me," written and sung by Chuck Berry (Chess Records, 1956); "Come Together" (*Abbey*

Road version), Lennon and McCartney, sung by the Beatles (Apple Records, 1969); Maynard Ferguson, "Big Bop Nouveau" (2005).

15. "Duck v. Tree": written in collaboration with Ken Henry, a good friend. Ken is a University of Oregon fan, and I went to Stanford.

16. "Nosey Mouse", stories written by Mayme "Mimi" Frommeyer, "Fun Fair for the Forest Friends" (circa 1968), "The Adventures of Ginger & Candy" (circa 1960): Mimi was my grandmother (my mom's mom). Mimi was one of the strongest women I've known. In the 1930s and '40s she was the children's clothes buyer for Pogue's Department Store (H. & S. Pogue Company) in Cincinnati, Ohio. I remember Mimi telling me stories about when she would travel to New York (by train) to buy children's clothes for Pogue's. She had a lot of responsibility. Mimi raised two daughters in Cincinnati; worked as a professional in a competitive, male-dominated retail business; and sent both her kids to college. She was doing stuff in the '30s and '40s that women generally didn't think of doing until the mid-'60s. Mimi was an amazing woman.

17. "No Santa Claus!", "No Santa Claus?": Read together, these two poems combine as a reverso poem (see Endnote No. 9).

18. "Snow Bound (*a Christmas Holiday*)", verses 3, 4 and 5: inspired by "November," Mary Oliver, *Why I Wake Early, New Poems by Mary Oliver* (Boston: Beacon Press, 2004), 63; Currier & Ives, "Winter Pastime" (1855); Currier & Ives, "Winter Morning" (1861); Currier & Ives, "Home to Thanksgiving" (1867); "The Christmas Song" (1945) lyrics by Robert Wells and Mel Tormé, music by Mel Tormé, sung and recorded by Nat King Cole.

19. "Looking at a Ringed Moon on New Year's Eve": This poem follows the rhyme scheme of "Stopping by Woods on a Snowy Evening" by Robert Frost (1874–1963). It was written for Lizanne and Fred after one of their New Year's Eve parties.

20. Progress Report of Mary Melanson, Grade 5, Seattle Public Schools, View Ridge School, Ms. Annabel Black, teacher, June 15, 1956: This is Ms. Black's fifth-grade graduation note written to Mary. In her note, Ms. Black recognizes Mary's "pioneer spirit." On many occasions, Mary mentioned how Ms. Black influenced her life and considered her "the best teacher" she ever had. Ms. Black's note reads as follows:

> Dear Mary,
>
> You have the wonderful ability to look life right smack in the eye and not back up a foot. You have lots of courage. Yours is the pioneer spirit. Never lose this ability Mary, as life will never defeat you.
>
> Remember to be gentle with others as all do not have your toughness of spirit. Also remember to accept love that people offer you for this is the secret of happiness.
>
> Love,
>
> Annabel Black

21. "Mary's Song": The poem I read at Mary's Memorial Service, January 28, 2017. I thank the following for reading Scripture at Mary's Service: Sue Perez, Mary's youngest sister, for reading "The Shepherd's Prayer" (Psalm 23); Christopher Lococo, Mary's and my friend and son of John and Sandi Lococo, for reading Mt 5:1–2, 6:25–33; and Jessica Dykhouse, Mary's and my niece, for reading 1 Cor 13:4–13. Thank you Sandi Lococo, Mary's good friend, for reading your "Remembrances of Mary." My thanks to the Stone Church Chancel Choir, Director Nancy Kromm, Mark Bruce, organist, and Beverly Blount, guest pianist and vocalist, for helping celebrate Mary's life. Rev. Irene Pak Lee, thank you so much for your homily to Mary, "Goodness and Mercy and Love will Follow."

22. "Reflections on a Himalayan Urn": John Keats (1795–1821) wrote "Ode on a Grecian Urn" from which several ideas, thoughts and phrases are alluded to in "Reflections."

22a. "Reflections," stanza two, lines 5-10: the following lines from "Ode on a Grecian Urn" are referenced:

> ". . . to whom thou say'st,
>
> 'Beauty is truth, truth beauty,'—that is all
>
> Ye know on earth, and all ye need to know."

23. "Beloved": Calligraphy by Jeanette Rapp. Claudia Hamm framed this poem. The poem was written as a Lenten devotional for Stone Church of Willow Glen. The Church's theme for Lent that year was "Walking with Jesus." The song, "I Want Jesus to Walk with Me," sung by Eric Bibb, influenced this poem. The poem reads as follows:

Beloved

With every precious breath you take,
With measured beat your heart doth make,
With step and stride though body aches,
Know I'll love you evermore.

You are my wife, my love, my friend,
I'll comfort you 'til winter's end,
For all my love you can depend,
And know I'll love you evermore.

We've walked with Jesus to this day,
His comfort sought without dismay,
He's bound our hearts as we have prayed,
And our love has deepened evermore.

As life's journey does draw nigh,
No mournful tears do either cry,
For together we'll be on Heaven's high,
And our love will be forevermore—
Our love will be forevermore.

24. "parsley, sage, rosemary, and thyme" is the refrain of the traditional English ballad, "Scarborough Fair." The ballad has a long and rich history and can trace its origin to the mid-1600's. A modern version of "Scarborough Fair" is the title tract of Simon & Garfunkel's album *Parsley, Sage, Rosemary and Thyme* (Columbia Records, 1966).

25. "Father, we thank You for the night": Mary's family's table grace, adapted from the children's prayer written by Rebecca J. Weston (1885). Mary and I shared this short, simple prayer before the many evening meals we enjoyed together. Weston's prayer follows:

    Father, we thank thee for the night,
    and for the pleasant morning light;
    for rest and food and loving care,
    and all that makes the day so fair.

    Help us to do the things we should,
    to be to others kind and good;
    in all we do, in work or play,
    to grow more loving every day.

26. "The Shepherd's Prayer" (Psalm 23): Mary always referred to Psalm 23 as "The Shepherd's Prayer." The following sources are referenced: Psalm 23; 1 Chron 29:10–18; Mt 6:9–15; Lk 11:1–2; Phil 4:8; Rev. Dr. Paul Watermulder, Presbyterian Church of Los Gatos, "Freedom, Family and Faith," July 7, 2019 sermon, pclg.org/sermons (6:27); Ben Keyes, "'For Your Name's Sake'—Living for the Reputation of God," L'Abri Fellowship, Southborough, Massachusetts, Resources, February 11, 2020, February 7, 2020 lecture to 1:25:45, https://southboroughlabri.org/; Sarah Chestnut, L'Abri Fellowship, Home Chapel Service, May 27, 2020 at 21:00–25:50, https://www.facebook.com/sborolabri/.

27. "You Restore My Soul": Psalm 23:2–3. Geographically, this beach is Rio del Mar Beach named for the small crossroads, coastal

community of Rio. Capitola Beach fronts the small, beach town of Capitola, located about three miles west of Rio, across Soquel Cove of Monterey Bay. Mary and I always called Rio Beach, Capitola Beach.

28. "The Vineyard *(a one-act poem in four scenes)*": Inspired by the winery, vineyard and writing of Tom Kruse, friend, farmer and winemaker of Thomas Kruse Winery and Claire's Field Vineyard, Gilroy, California.

29. "On the Kingdom of God, an Open Bible and My Dad": Written for a Bible study class taught by Rev. Dr. Art Mills, former pastor of Stone Church of Willow Glen. At the conclusion of the class, Art asked us to write a short piece on how we had experienced the Kingdom of God and share it with the class. Art was Pastor of Stone Church from 1996 to 2005.

Photo Credits and Notes

Dust jacket, front cover: Clockface, *Grandad's Old Clock*, photo by Michael Breuleux, January 2024.

Page iii: *Grandad's Old Clock*, photo by Michael Breuleux, May 2021. My thanks to Jason Lorist, owner of The Tick Tock Shop, Santa Clara, California, for the maintenance and repair of *Grandad's Old Clock* and for keeping the *Old Clock* running. Jason is an "old school" craftsman and clocksmith and I thank him for his work.

Page 2: Pendulum, *Grandad's Old Clock*, photo by Michael Breuleux, April 2023.

Page 8: Eugene Albert "Grandad" Frommeyer with his two granddaughters, Betty Rae and Jean, Hyde Park, Cincinnati, Ohio, photographer unknown, circa 1939.

Page 39: Bakhmut, Ukraine, photographer unknown, February 2023.

Page 41: Smith Mountain Lake, Virginia, photo by Rev. Dr. Ken Henry, 2020.

Page 44: Grand Oak of Montgomery Hill Park, San José, California, photo by Michael Breuleux, 2007.

Page 57: The Old Bar, Longfellow's Wayside Inn, Sudbury, Massachusetts, photographer unknown.

Page 69: Mary, Company Halloween Party, Cardiometrics, Inc., Mountain View, California, photographer unknown, 1987.

Page 80: Mimi, photo most probably taken by my mom, Betsy Breuleux, or my dad, Fritz Breuleux, Walnut Creek, California, circa 1966.

Page 83: Ginger & Candy, watercolor prints by J. Scherer.

Page 85: Holidays, *Grandad's Old Clock* ~ Christmas 2016, photo by Michael Breuleux, December 2016; cover design by Bublish, Inc.

Page 88: Mary & Mike, Christmas 1996, photo by Melody Casagranda, Mary's twin sister, San José, California, December 1996.

Page 93: Angel, tile detail of *azulejo* frieze on the grand double staircase that ascends Monte de São Estevão to the baroque chapel of Nossa Senhora dos Remédios, Lamego, Portugal, photograph by Alice Bailey, April 2017.

Page 99: Mary's Fifth Grade Progress Report, graduation note written by Ms. Annabel Black, teacher, June 15, 1956.

Page 104: The Book Club, photo by Michael Breuleux, July 17, 2015.

Page 107: *Stengel Beach at Sea Ranch, California's Mendocino Coast*, 12" x 18" acrylic, 2017; artist: Lynden Keith Johnson; commissioned by Michael Breuleux in memory of Mary Elizabeth Breuleux (1945–2016).

Page 108: Urn, Stengel Beach, Sea Ranch, California, photo by Michael Breuleux, June 26, 2017.

Page 113: Stained glass window, Stone Church Sanctuary, Willow Glen, California, photo by Michael Breuleux, Sunday afternoon, May 8, 2017.

Page 120: *Christ Washing the Feet of the Apostles,* Meister des Hausbuches (Master of the Housebook) 1475. It has been suggested that Erhard Reuwich of Utrecht, Netherlands is the Housebook Master. Art scholars, however, have not universally accepted this view.

Page 134: *Peace* or *The Expanding Universe*, 93-foot (28 m) sculpture created by Beniamino "Bene" Bufano (1890–1970) in collaboration with Alfonso Pardiñas of Byzantine Mosaics; placed behind Timber Cove Lodge overlooking the Pacific Ocean and located approximately eighteen miles south of Sea Ranch; the work was started in 1962 and completed in 1969; photograph by Michael Breuleux, June 2017.

Page 139: Mary & Mike, photo by Melody Casagranda, Mary's twin sister, Clear Lake, California, June 2012.

Page 143: Urn, Stengel Beach, Sea Ranch, California, Communion Bread baked by Mary Johnson, a good friend; photo by Michael Breuleux, June 26, 2017.

Dust jacket, back flap: photo by Fred Oliver, 2023.

www.ingramcontent.com/pod-product-compliance
Lightning Source LLC
Chambersburg PA
CBHW061151170426
43209CB00044B/1990/J